D0459710

TRIBES OF THE
SOUTHERN PLAINS

✜

TIME®
LIFE
BOOKS

Other Publications
THE TIME-LIFE COMPLETE GARDENER
THE NEW HOME REPAIR AND IMPROVEMENT
JOURNEY THROUGH THE MIND AND BODY
WEIGHT WATCHERS® SMART CHOICE RECIPE COLLECTION
TRUE CRIME
THE ART OF WOODWORKING
LOST CIVILIZATIONS
ECHOES OF GLORY
THE NEW FACE OF WAR
HOW THINGS WORK
WINGS OF WAR
CREATIVE EVERYDAY COOKING
COLLECTOR'S LIBRARY OF THE UNKNOWN
CLASSICS OF WORLD WAR II
TIME-LIFE LIBRARY OF CURIOUS AND UNUSUAL FACTS
AMERICAN COUNTRY
VOYAGE THROUGH THE UNIVERSE
THE THIRD REICH
MYSTERIES OF THE UNKNOWN
TIME FRAME
FIX IT YOURSELF
FITNESS, HEALTH & NUTRITION
SUCCESSFUL PARENTING
HEALTHY HOME COOKING
UNDERSTANDING COMPUTERS
LIBRARY OF NATIONS
THE ENCHANTED WORLD
THE KODAK LIBRARY OF CREATIVE PHOTOGRAPHY
GREAT MEALS IN MINUTES
THE CIVIL WAR
PLANET EARTH
COLLECTOR'S LIBRARY OF THE CIVIL WAR
THE EPIC OF FLIGHT
THE GOOD COOK
WORLD WAR II
THE OLD WEST

*For information on and a full description of any of the Time-Life Books
series listed above, please call 1-800-621-7026 or write:*
Reader Information
Time-Life Customer Service
P.O. Box C-32068
Richmond, Virginia 23261-2068

This volume is one of a series that chronicles the history and culture of the Native Americans. Other books in the series include:

The Cover: Jim Two Hatchet, a Kiowa leader, poses in traditional garb in this portrait from 1898. Two Hatchet actively opposed the land allotment programs imposed on the Kiowa by the United States government and fought to keep Indian reservation land in communal ownership.

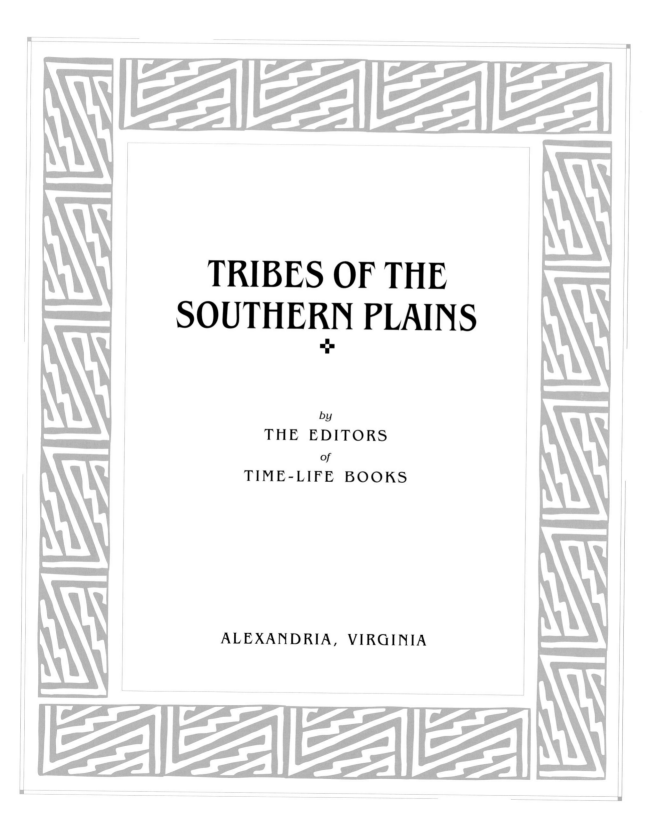

TRIBES OF THE SOUTHERN PLAINS

✤

by
THE EDITORS
of
TIME-LIFE BOOKS

ALEXANDRIA, VIRGINIA

Time-Life Books is a division of Time Life Inc.

PRESIDENT and CEO: John M. Fahey Jr.

TIME-LIFE BOOKS

MANAGING EDITOR: Roberta Conlan

Director of Design: Michael Hentges
Director of Editorial Operations: Ellen Robling
Director of Photography and Research: John Conrad Weiser
Senior Editors: Russell B. Adams Jr., Dale M. Brown, Janet Cave, Lee Hassig, Robert Somerville, Henry Woodhead
Special Projects Editor: Rita Thievon Mullin
Director of Technology: Eileen Bradley
Library: Louise D. Forstall

PRESIDENT: John D. Hall

Vice President, Director of Marketing: Nancy K. Jones
Vice President, Director of New Product Development: Neil Kagan
Vice President, Book Production: Marjann Caldwell
Production Manager: Marlene Zack
Quality Assurance Manager: Miriam P. Newton

THE AMERICAN INDIANS

SERIES EDITOR: Henry Woodhead
Administrative Editor: Loretta Y. Britten

Editorial Staff for *Tribes of the Southern Plains*
Senior Art Director: Dale Pollekoff
Art Director: Mary Gasperetti
Picture Editor: Jane Coughran
Text Editors: Stephen G. Hyslop (principal), Denise Dersin, John Newton
Associate Editors/Research-Writing: Robert H. Wooldridge Jr. (principal), Jennifer Veech
Senior Copyeditor: Ann Lee Bruen
Picture Coordinator: Daryl Beard
Editorial Assistant: Christine Higgins

Special Contributors: Amy Aldrich, Ronald H. Bailey, George Daniels, Maggie Debelius, Marilyn Murphy Terrell (text); Elizabeth Schleichert, (research-writing); Martha Lee Beckington, Sarah Labouisse, Anne Whittle (research); Barbara L. Klein (index).

Correspondents: Christine Hinze (London), Christina Lieberman (New York), Maria Vincenza Aloisi (Paris). Valuable assistance was also provided by: Barbara Gevene Hertz (Copenhagen), Elizabeth Brown (New York).

General Consultants
Willard H. Rollings is an associate professor of history at the University of Nevada, Las Vegas, where he teaches courses in the ethnohistory of Native Americans and the history of the Trans-Mississippi West. A specialist in southern Plains peoples, Dr. Rollings focuses his research on the political, economic, and social history of the Osage and other southern Plains peoples. He is the author of *The Osage: An Ethnohistorical Study of Hegemony on the Prairie-Plains* and *The Comanche*. Dr. Rollings, who is part Choctaw and Cherokee, has been a fellow of the Newberry Library's D'Arcy McNickle Center for the History of the American Indian.

Frederick E. Hoxie is academic vice president for the Newberry Library in Chicago and former director of its D'Arcy McNickle Center for the History of the American Indian. Dr. Hoxie is the author of *A Final Promise: The Campaign to Assimilate the Indians 1880-1920* and other works. He has served as a history consultant to the Cheyenne River and Standing Rock Sioux tribes, Little Big Horn College archives, and the Senate Select Committee on Indian Affairs. He is a trustee of the National Museum of the American Indian in Washington, D.C.

Candace Green has a Ph.D in anthropology from the University of Oklahoma. She holds the position of specialist for North American ethnology in the Department of Anthropology at the Smithsonian Institution's National Museum of Natural History. Her field of specialty is Plains Indian art, with particular emphasis on southern Plains graphic art and on concepts of the ownership of designs.

© 1995 Time Life Inc. All rights reserved. No part of this book may be reproduced in any form or by any electronic or mechanical means, including information storage and retrieval devices or systems, without prior written permission from the publisher, except that brief passages may be quoted for reviews.
First printing. Printed in U.S.A.
Published simultaneously in Canada.
School and library distribution by Time-Life Education, P.O. Box 85026, Richmond, Virginia 23285-5026.
Time-Life is a trademark of Time Warner Inc. U.S.A.

Library of Congress Cataloging in Publication Data
Tribes of the southern plains/by the editors of Time-Life Books.
    p.   cm.—(The American Indians)
    Includes bibliographical references and index.
    ISBN 0-8094-9595-3
    1. Indians of North America—Great Plains—History. 2. Indians of North America—Southwest, New—History. 3. Indians of North America—Great Plains—Social life and customs. 4. Indians of North America—Southwest, New—Social life and customs. I. Time-Life Books. II. Series.
E78.G73T73 1995   95-8790
978'.00497—dc20   CIP

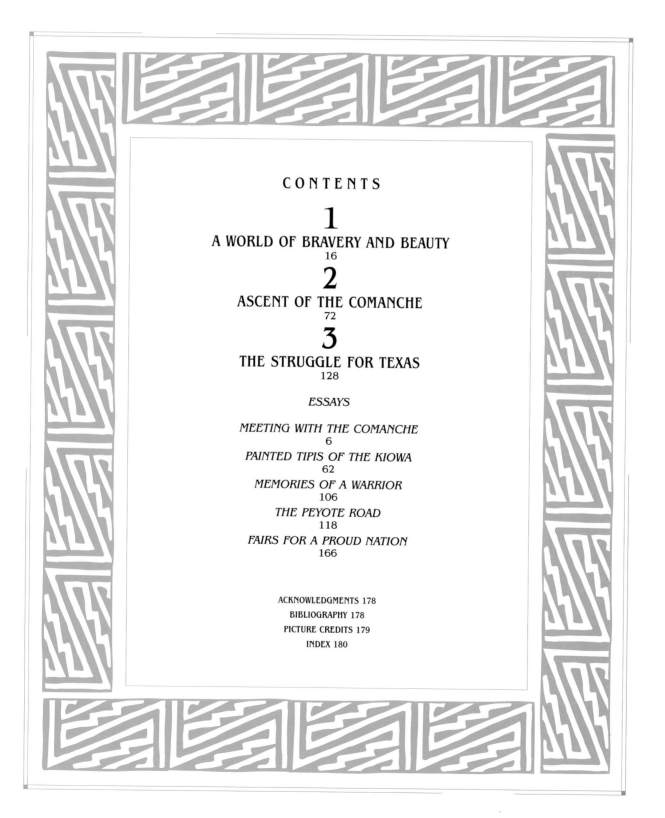

CONTENTS

1
A WORLD OF BRAVERY AND BEAUTY

2
ASCENT OF THE COMANCHE

3
THE STRUGGLE FOR TEXAS

ESSAYS

MEETING WITH THE COMANCHE

In 1834 artist George Catlin accompanied a U.S. Cavalry regiment on a peacekeeping expedition across the southern Plains. Catlin called the journey the "first grand *civilized foray* into the country of the wild and warlike Comanches." Like most of his contemporaries, he had much to learn about the tribe. Comanches were indeed avid warriors, but they owed their success not to "wild"

Wielding lances and shields, mounted Comanche warriors demonstrate their skills for Catlin. The artist was awed by the warriors' agility, pronouncing them "the most extraordinary horsemen that I have seen yet in all my travels." Comanche shields like the one above, depicting the sun and stars and adorned with eagle feathers and horsehair, were said to confer protective powers on their warrior owners.

instinct but to well-developed skills, and they could be as hospitable to strangers as they were harsh to enemies. What Catlin called Comanche country was not their ancestral homeland. They had come to the southern Plains from the Rockies, lured by bison and other game that abounded on the grasslands. There they amassed herds of horses and prospered as hunters, traders, and raiders.

Catlin's party soon learned that Comanches were adept at making peace as well as war. Approaching a village under a white flag, the soldiers were met by men displaying a white buffalo skin. "To the everlasting credit of the Comanches," wrote Catlin, they came out "without a weapon of any kind, to meet a war party bristling with arms and trespassing to the middle of their country."

Thus welcomed, Catlin freely observed the Comanches at home and on the trail and made sketches that he later converted into paintings. Reproduced here along with tribal artifacts, these scenes testify to the grace and expertise that marked all aspects of Comanche life, from everyday tasks to mortal combat.

REWARDS OF THE HUNT

Well-armed Comanches chase down buffalo on the rolling grasslands. Comanche horses were carefully bred and trained, for they had to be as agile as their riders to avoid disaster in the fast-paced, intricate moves of the hunt.

Women stretch and scrape buffalo hides in a base camp of the sort Comanche bands often formed during buffalo hunts. Catlin noted that "the valley, for a mile distant about the village, seemed speckled with horses and mules."

Hide scrapers such as this one, with a handle of elk bone and an iron blade, were used by Comanche women to clean skins. Comanches often decorated tanned hides with a radiating emblem (far right) that Catlin called "a most wonderfully painted sun."

LIFE ON THE MOVE

A fracas erupts among dogs and their owners as Comanches break camp, their possessions piled on travois drawn by their animals. For the Comanche, who seldom stayed in one place for long, moving could be a trying experience. Catlin noted that quarrels commenced "usually amongst the dogs" and spread to the women who supervised them.

Comanches spent long hours on horseback and valued good saddles like this one, made for a woman and crafted of rawhide stretched over wood. Comanche baby carriers (below) were heavily padded and often strapped to the saddle.

THE CEREMONY OF WARFARE

Comanches seek good fortune in war by galloping toward a bluff said to be inhabited by powerful spirits and then "sacrificing their best arrow," as Catlin put it. Comanche warriors cherished their bows and arrows and carried them in style, as evidenced by the splendid fur quiver and bow case above.

Racing at top speed, a Comanche warrior prepares to thrust his 14-foot-long lance into a rival Osage. Long after they obtained firearms, Comanches continued to fight with lances like the steel-tipped one shown in a feathered sheath at top left. Warriors liked the lance because it tested a man's strength and brought him in touch with his enemy.

An adopted captive named Jesús Sánchez displays the full panoply of the Comanche fighting man. Born in Spanish territory, Sánchez was raised by Comanches and became one of his band's leading warriors. Catlin was impressed by his "gentlemanly politeness and friendship."

1

A WORLD OF BRAVERY AND BEAUTY

Kiowa warrior Tape-day-ah wears the fur cap of the Onde, the tribe's elite class, in this photograph taken about 1870. A great fighting man, Tape-day-ah was a member of every known Kiowa raiding party between 1870 and 1874.

Long ago, according to a tale related by Kiowas of the southern Plains, a warrior was returning from a raid against distant enemies when he became separated from his companions and had to find his way back home on his own. The summer sun beat down fiercely, and the path he followed over the rolling prairie was hard and dry. Tormented by thirst, he consoled himself with thoughts of the welcome that awaited him from his friends and family members in camp, which lay far beyond the horizon.

Then, as the sun dipped toward the west, he heard a voice nearby, chanting a song as clear and fresh as a murmuring stream. Drawn by the mysterious music, the warrior climbed to the top of a ridge and peered over the rim. There below, he saw "a beautiful red wolf at the bottom of a grassy ravine," in the words of Kiowa storyteller James Auchiah. "Red Wolf held in his right paw a gourd that he shook with a pulsating movement. His body moved rhythmically up and down in tempo with the beautiful songs pouring from his long, lean throat."

The warrior stood entranced on the hilltop through the night, drinking in song after song. When dawn arrived, Red Wolf spoke to his delighted listener. "I have given you a new dance with many beautiful songs," he explained. "This is a gift for you to take to your people."

Renewed by this miraculous encounter, the warrior continued his journey and reached the Kiowa encampment before the day was out. There he told his people of the gift Red Wolf had bequeathed to them. The songs and dances he passed along to them became part of a ceremony called the Gourd Dance, performed by the tribe each summer.

In honor of the lone warrior who beheld Red Wolf, the ritual was entrusted to a society of respected hunters and soldiers. Each year, those men would begin the dance, but after a while, women would join in, for the occasion celebrated both bravery and beauty—the power and grace that came to all Kiowas who kept faith with their ancestral powers. As the drum thundered and the songs poured forth, the spirits of the dancers and of all those in attendance took flight and soared. Kiowas never failed to honor the creature who taught them this stirring ritual of renewal. "To show their appreciation to Red Wolf," notes the storyteller, the dancers to this day end each song "with a wolf cry and a special shake of their gourds."

The Indians of the southern Plains have always cared as much for spiritual gifts, like the songs and dances acquired by this legendary Kiowa warrior, as for worldly gains. To be sure, they long prided themselves on their prowess as hunters and warriors, for they inhabited a boundless country, roamed by herds of buffalo that drew neighboring groups into frequent conflict. For them as for Indians elsewhere, however, hunting and warfare were uplifting. Men who overcame adversity and outwitted their prey emerged stronger in spirit.

The land that inspired such daring and devotion belonged to everyone—and to no one. Neither the Kiowa nor the Comanche, with whom they became allied, were native to the southern Plains. They came down from the north and vied with other intruders in the new territory. Among those who preceded them were adventurers from New Spain, or Mexico. Much like the Indians, those Spaniards trusted that their God would grant them earthly success, and that success would in turn make them worthier in the eyes of the faithful. In their case, the lure was not buffalo but the elusive promise of gold and silver—treasure they wanted to claim for Spain and deny to their European rivals.

The gold-hungry masters of New Spain had been searching northward for fortune without success since the mid-1500s. That quest had led them first to New Mexico, where they subjugated the Pueblo peoples but found no trace of the bastions of wealth they sought—the fabled seven golden cities of Cíbola, whose legend went back to the Dark Ages. Some of the Indians the Spaniards encountered in New Mexico attempted to distract them with tales of a distant domain called Quivira, said to be so awash in riches that commoners there drank from bowls of pure gold. Probing eastward from the Rio Grande, the conquistadors Francisco Vásquez de Coronado in 1541 and Juan de Oñate in 1601 both searched fruitlessly on the Plains for Quivira and its trove.

Subsequently, Spanish imaginations were fired by tales of yet another golden realm—"el gran reyno de los Texas," the great kingdom of Texas, a palatial domain so close to Quivira, it was said, that the two peoples visited back and forth regularly. As before, the Spaniards were doomed to dis-

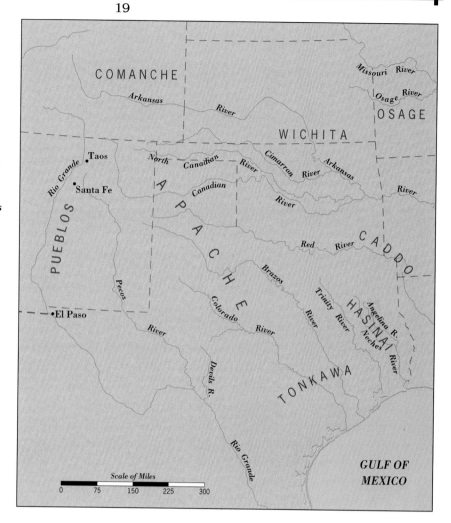

Dominated by rolling grasslands, the southern Plains are fringed by mixed woodlands and prairie to the east and by desert to the south and west. When Europeans met with tribes here in the late 1600s, roving Apaches controlled much of the region. Tonkawas ranged to their south, and Wichitas, Hasinais, and Caddos farmed the prairie to their east. Osages from the Ohio Valley were filtering into southwestern Missouri and Comanches were coming down from the Rockies to the Arkansas River area, but Kiowas had yet to appear from the north.

appointment. An expedition dispatched in 1683 found no sign of that great kingdom. A second party set forth in 1689, led by Alonso de León and a Catholic priest, Father Damián Mazanet. Adding urgency to their quest was a report that the rival French had recently established a fort on the Gulf Coast. Heading east across the Plains, the Spaniards encountered Indians calling out what Mazanet took to be the words *Techas! Techas!* Farther on, near the Neches River, they were cordially greeted by the chief of a prosperous tribe called the Nabedache. The explorers jubilantly reported to their superiors that they had at last discovered the kingdom of Texas and befriended its ruler.

But this hasty assessment was soon amended. Before they returned to New Mexico, de León and Mazanet established a mission in east Texas among the Nabedache. The priest they left behind, Father Francisco Casañas, came to view the situation more soberly. In 1691 he asserted that the chief of the Nabedache was no king, that his tribe was just one of several in the area, known collectively by the name Hasinai. The term Techas, or *Texias,* as he put it, simply meant "friends and applies to all the friendly tribes, although their languages may be different."

Casañas enumerated 48 such tribes living across a 500-mile expanse that extended from the Rio Grande in the west to the Red River in what is now Louisiana. "Kingdom this might be called, and a very large one," added Casañas, "if these friendly tribes had a head who governs them all. But this they have not. They say very appropriately that they were Texias, because they are friends of all the rest."

Although this country contained neither palaces nor precious metals, the Spaniards still hoped to colonize it, if only as a buffer against the hated French. The rivalries of the region's Indians were just as stubborn. The Hasinai may have been friendly with their immediate neighbors, but they had powerful foes in the area even before the Comanche and Kiowa arrived—notably the Wichita and Osage to their north. Like the Hasinai, those tribes lived at the eastern edge of the Plains, where they planted crops and lived in permanent villages. Yet that did not keep them from making lengthy forays to hunt buffalo or raid their enemies. And out to the west in drier country lived the formidable Tonkawa and Apache—who depended in large part on the bison and opposed all those who infringed on their prized hunting grounds.

In the years to come, Europeans would contribute significantly to tribal conflict in the region by introducing the horse and the gun. The horse, in particular, would alter the lives of the Native Americans and open the way for the influx of Comanches and Kiowas into the area. The Comanche, by far the larger of the two groups, would prove to be especially formidable on horseback, and for a long interval they would dominate the southern Plains, defying both Spaniards and Anglo-Americans and acquiring a reputation as fierce marauders. Yet these keen Indian intruders were not so different in character from their white foes. Like the Europeans, they were proud and opportunistic, staunchly protective of their loved ones, and steeped in beliefs and rituals that strengthened them in their bold pursuits.

The southern Plains—the domain that lured the Comanche and other ambitious peoples from their distant homelands—was bordered to the north by the Arkansas River and to the east by the woodlands that blanketed what is now Missouri, Arkansas, and Louisiana and extended into neighboring parts of Kansas, Oklahoma, and Texas. From there westward, the grasslands rolled on for hundreds of miles before fetching up against the mountains of New Mexico and Colorado. On that vast and open stage, a drama of relentless competition was played out.

Life was never easy here. Only the region's eastern fringe, with up to 40 inches of rain annually, sustained much in the way of farming. In the central area, annual precipitation fell off to about 20 inches, with near-desert conditions prevailing in the far Southwest.

Many rivers crossed the southern Plains, but they were often cloudy and unpalatable. Midsummer brought intense heat and winds that blew from the south like furnace blasts, shriveling vegetation and all but searing the skin. Winters were milder here than to the north, but temperatures sometimes dipped below zero, with howling "northers" that one traveler described as a "mad, rushing combination of wind and snow which neither man nor beast could face. Persons lost upon the prairie were almost certain to meet with death."

And there were other seasonal scourges, from pounding hailstorms to pulverizing tornadoes. A legend related by the Kiowa people says that the first twister came about when ancient tribespeople attempted to mold a horse from clay. The beast took shape, recounted one storyteller, but it was a terrible thing: "It began to writhe, slowly at first, then faster and faster until there was a great commotion everywhere. The wind grew up and carried everything away. The Kiowas were afraid of that awful thing and they went running about, talking to it. And at last it was calm." Ever after, when the black clouds began to swirl, Kiowas knew the monster was approaching: "Lightning comes from its mouth, and the tail, whipping and thrashing on the air, makes the high, hot wind." Kiowas speak to it, saying, "Pass over me." And in time, it does.

Here and there on the southern Plains, trees offered shelter from the hostile elements. On the eastern borders, fingers of deciduous forest crept out onto the level lands; and lining the river bottoms throughout were groves of oak, elm, willow, and cottonwood. Elsewhere the land stretched on without relief, except for occasional ridges and ravines. Along the upper Red River and a few other rugged spots, the cliffs were steep. There bands of Indians sometimes camped down in the canyons to evade the winter wind or pursuing enemies.

What drew tribes to the region in spite of its many hardships were the magnificent grasslands and the numerous creatures that they sustained. In the more humid east thrived the deep-rooted tall grasses, some reaching as high as eight feet. Beyond, in drier conditions, flourished the short grasses, blanketing the earth with a thick sod.

The majority of the animals on the Plains were grass or seed eaters and obtained the moisture they needed primarily from their forage. Among them were scurrying pin-tailed grouse and prairie chickens, and immense flocks of cranes, geese, and ducks that paused at the region's

ART OF THE ANCIENTS

This stretch of the lower Pecos River was visited for thousands of years by Indian bands who covered the cliff faces with images of transcendent power. More than 300 rock art sites have been found in the area.

In southwest Texas, where the Pecos River enters the Rio Grande, lies one of the richest collections of ancient rock art in North America. For roughly 4,000 years before Europeans reached the area, Indians painted designs on the walls of canyons carved by these rivers and other natural forces.

Much of what is known about the bands that gathered here comes from their paintings. They were keen hunters as well as gatherers and fervently portrayed many of the creatures they encountered on their forays, including deer, bison, and the dreaded panther.

More mysterious are figures in the paintings with human attributes or the combined features of humans and animals. These haunting images may well represent shamans, or medicine men. Shamans loomed large in the lives of early hunter-gatherers because they interceded for people with their prey, divining the location of game and appeasing the animal spirits. Shamans assumed the guise of animals in ceremonies—and some of them claimed the ability to do so in real life as well. Many of these rock paintings were probably inspired by shamans and figured in rituals that brought people in touch with the spirits and their powers.

Some of the paintings are vast in scale—up to 12 feet high and 30 feet across—and required collaborative effort. They may have been outlined by a master painter and filled in by assistants standing on ladders or scaffolding to reach remote spots. In many places, the artists covered old images with new ones, suggesting that fresh paintings were needed to appeal to the spirits.

The spell of these paintings was ultimately broken by intruders. Among the most recent pictures are scenes telling of the arrival of Europeans—who brought an end to the way of life that produced these compelling images.

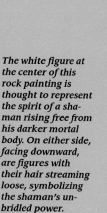

Painted pebbles like this predate the earliest known cliff paintings in the Pecos area by a few thousand years. Their abstract designs likely had spiritual significance.

The white figure at the center of this rock painting is thought to represent the spirit of a shaman rising free from his darker mortal body. On either side, facing downward, are figures with their hair streaming loose, symbolizing the shaman's unbridled power.

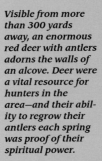

Visible from more than 300 yards away, an enormous red deer with antlers adorns the walls of an alcove. Deer were a vital resource for hunters in the area—and their ability to regrow their antlers each spring was proof of their spiritual power.

A human figure confronts a standing buffalo with human hands and feet in a rock painting that may represent a shaman taking on the guise of a bison. Buffalo ranged in the Pecos area during wetter periods in early times, and shamans may have conducted rituals to lure them within reach of hunters.

Flanked on both sides by huge panthers, a shaman figure with the pointed ears of a cat holds the creatures at bay with arms outstretched. Communing with the panther—the fiercest predator in the area—was the supreme demonstration of a shaman's power.

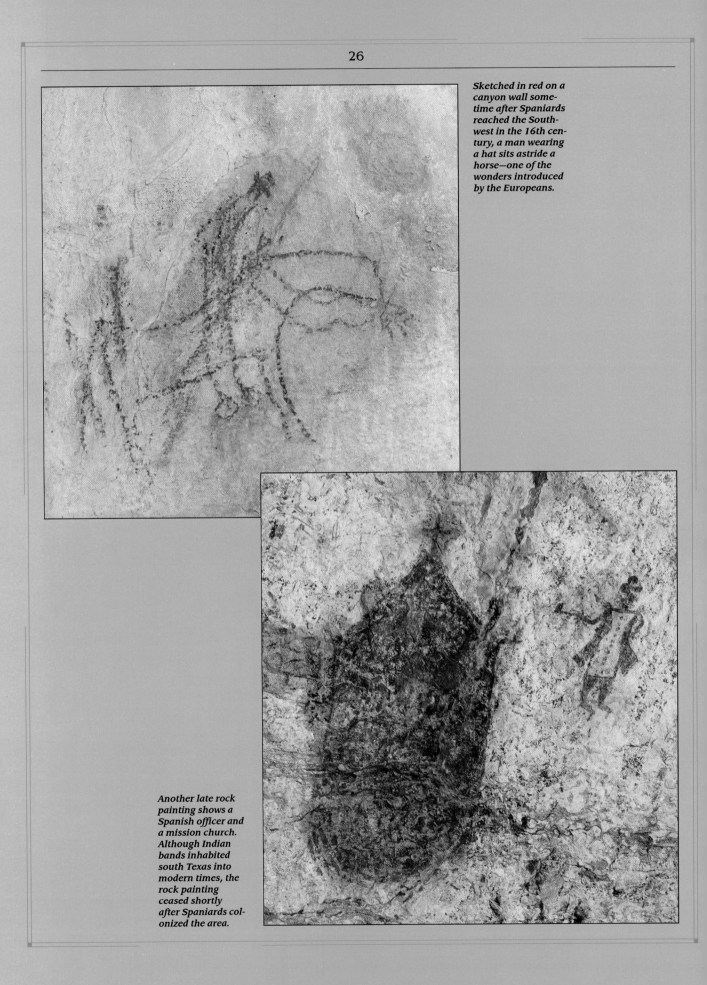

Sketched in red on a canyon wall sometime after Spaniards reached the Southwest in the 16th century, a man wearing a hat sits astride a horse—one of the wonders introduced by the Europeans.

Another late rock painting shows a Spanish officer and a mission church. Although Indian bands inhabited south Texas into modern times, the rock painting ceased shortly after Spaniards colonized the area.

waterways on their way to and from their northern breeding grounds. Jack rabbits abounded, but they were as nothing compared to the prairie dogs that congregated in sprawling towns, harboring tens of millions of animals. Those prodigious colonies helped sustain the majestic predators that inspired the native Plains dwellers—the soaring eagles and hawks, and the cunning coyotes, wolves, and foxes.

Among the larger denizens of the region were the fleet pronghorn antelope, and in wooded areas, deer and elk. Yet the most important quarry for the Indians was the bison, which sometimes convened in herds covering up to 50 square miles and containing as many as 500,000 animals. Bison supplied the Indians with vast stores of meat and almost all the other essentials of life, from sheltering tipis to warm clothing, handy implements, and even bone-rattle toys for the infants.

In time, Indian hunting bands would profit by the introduction of horses and begin to range freely across the short-grass country, where the larger bison herds congregated. When the Spaniards first arrived, however, the people of the southern Plains traveled on foot, and relatively few made their home on the open grasslands. Most ventured there once or twice a year to hunt, then returned to their villages amid the woods and tall-grass clearings to the east, where they raised corn and other crops.

Among those energetic farming peoples were the confederated Hasinai whom the Spaniards encountered in southeast Texas in the late 1600s. Members of the Caddoan language family, they were sometimes referred to as Caddos, although that term also applied to Caddoan speakers of Louisiana and Arkansas who formed similar but distinct confederacies. The Hasinai had ties to the Mississippian mound-building culture of earlier times. Like the Mississippians, they cleared village sites along the forested banks of rivers and streams, where silt deposited by floods over the eons offered fertile ground for their gardens. The eight small tribes of the Hasinai—each consisting of several affiliated villages—lived along a 70-mile stretch of the converging Neches and Angelina Rivers. They were a relatively dark-skinned people and tattooed their faces and bodies with intricate designs.

Like others at the edge of the Plains, the Hasinai were expert foragers as well as farmers. They caught fish, frogs, and turtles; snared rabbits and various rodents; and took partridges, quail, wild turkeys, and waterfowl, whose calls they were adept at imitating. Among the big game in the vicinity were black bears, wild hogs, and deer, which the hunters some-times stalked wearing the animal's hide and horns. Deer yielded venison as well as tanned skins for moccasins, leggings, shirts, skirts, and other articles of clothing; bears offered meat, fur, and fat, which Hasinais used as ointment and sometimes quaffed as a hot drink.

Hasinai villagers possessed a knowledge of the environment that extended well beyond their immediate horizons. The big bison herds were about four days' journey, or some 120 miles, to the west, where the tall-grass prairie yielded to short grass. Large parties of Hasinai hunters, employing dogs as beasts of burden, made the trip in early winter, when the bison were fat and prime. They brought back to the village generous stores of meat, which the women dried in the sun or over fires.

Yet meat remained secondary in the Hasinai diet. They were farmers above all and grew boun-tiful crops in the rich bottom lands. Men helped with some of the heavier tasks, such as clearing fields and preparing the soft soil with plows made of wood or the shoulder blade of a bison. Women did the rest, however, raising corn, beans, squash, sunflowers, melons, and tobacco, cherished both for daily use and for ceremonies.

In the mild climate, the Hasinai harvested two crops of corn a year, one in late May, the other in Sep-tember. The ears were either cooked and eaten fresh, or dried and shelled for grinding into flour, which was mixed with wa-ter and eaten as gruel or baked into a tortilla-like bread. Seed corn was preserved by smoking it and then storing it in ashes in order to discourage weevils. Women sometimes cooked beans and corn together as succo-tash. Ordinarily, however, Hasinais consumed their bounty one food at a time as it ripened. In early spring, string beans might be the main dish for an entire week; then would come fresh corn, next wild fruit such as plums and berries, followed in turn by melons and squashes, another crop of corn, and finally nuts and acorns.

Living arrangements were communal. The typical household unit consisted of several families, who occupied a round lodge measuring per-haps 60 feet across. The pole framework was covered by thick layers of tall grass, sometimes reinforced with mud. Inside, a fire was kept constantly alight in the central hearth, below the smoke hole. Around the hearth,

This clay jar from the late 17th cen-tury was crafted among the Quapaw, who settled along the lower Arkansas River near the Mis-sissippi. The dark, star-shaped objects represent scalps stretched on hoops.

each family had its own living space and belongings, including the basketry and pottery at which Hasinais excelled. The beds, fashioned of reed matting overlaid with buffalo skins, were commonly raised off the floor on posts. In winter, people sometimes kindled small fires under the pallets for extra warmth. Villagers came together as one to build the lodge for the householders and were duly rewarded with a feast. People also cooperated to construct the temples, which were similar to the houses but larger and were sometimes erected on flat-topped earthen mounds reminiscent of the Mississippian culture.

Communities were divided into clans, whose members lived in lodges clustered together, an arrangement that enabled them to offer one another mutual assistance. Father Casañas, who spent 15 months among the Hasinai, related that in "sickness these Indians visit and aid each other with great kindness, trying to give to the sick all possible consolation by

In a scene reconstructed by artist George Catlin, the French explorer René-Robert Cavelier de La Salle encounters a welcoming party of Hasinais in their east Texas village, dominated by beehive-shaped lodges covered with grass. Reports of La Salle's expedition here in 1686 spurred Spanish authorities to establish missions among the Hasinai.

taking them something nice to eat. Some of them present the trinkets they own."

This cooperative spirit was reinforced by a strong system of government. At the head of the confederacy was a paramount chief with the title of *xinesi*. The position was hereditary and always fell to a male, although some women among the Hasinai exercised great influence. Like Mississippian rulers, the paramount derived a great deal of his authority from his ability to communicate with the supreme power in heaven as well as with lesser spirits. This he accomplished through the agency of two mysterious *coconocis*—said to be young boys, sent by the supreme power to serve as intermediaries. No one, upon pain of death, was ever permitted to look upon those messengers, who were concealed within two small huts near the main temple (they probably existed in spirit only).

At tribal gatherings, the paramount related his dialogues with the boys, speaking in his own voice and in a falsetto to represent the two messengers. Sometimes he reported that they were angry and foretold crop failure or some other debacle unless the people reformed and heeded him.

At top, in a sketch made by George Catlin in 1834, fields of corn surround the grass lodges of a Wichita village located on the North Fork of the Red River in Oklahoma. As shown in the accompanying photograph from the late 19th century, Wichita lodges were sturdy structures meant to accommodate up to 10 people and to last many years.

The throng would vow to do so, and the paramount would pray on their behalf for bounty and health. Then his voice would grow high and thin, and he would speak for the boys, informing the people that if they behaved properly, their prayers would be answered.

Below the paramount ranked the *caddi,* or local chiefs, and they in turn commanded subchiefs and assistants, who helped enforce discipline, sometimes using supple switches to flick lazy people across the chest or shoulders. It was usually done with a light hand, however, and each community preserved a measure of autonomy. "There is no village, however weak and unhappy it may be, which is not regarded by the others as free and independent," wrote a Spanish observer in the mid-1700s. Preserving peace among the villages was the foremost concern, and any party disturbing that peace risked possible banishment.

Faced with formidable tribal competitors to their north and west, the Hasinai did not shrink from challenges. Warriors feasted and danced before going off to battle, collected scalps, and vented their anger by torturing captives. Prominent among their foes were the Wichita—a term that applied collectively to several related Caddoan-speaking groups, including the Taovaya, the Tawakoni, the Waco, and the Wichita proper. Sometime before Europeans appeared, the Wichita had broken away from their Caddo homeland in what is now southern Louisiana and migrated northward, ending up along the great bend of the Arkansas River in present-day Kansas. There they erected villages of round, grass-covered lodges, smaller than those of the Hasinai and housing only a single extended family instead of several. Their skill at farming greatly impressed Juan de Oñate, who encountered them in 1601. "The villages were surrounded on all sides by fields of maize," he reported. "The stalks of maize were as high as that of New Spain and in many places higher."

The Wichita were equally impressive in appearance, for they outdid even the Hasinai in bodily ornamentation. The men tattooed their faces to such an extent that they called themselves the "raccoon-eyed people" and covered their arms and chests with marks symbolizing war honors and success on the hunt. The women decorated their noses, mouths, and chins and tattooed three concentric circles around their breasts, which was said to keep them firm into old age.

Women dominated village life, with the oldest competent woman serving as "mother of the house." She and her kinswomen performed the majority of the domestic chores. As Frenchman Athanase de Mézières observed in the mid-1700s, "The women tan, sew, and paint the skins, fence

the cornfields, care for the cornfields, harvest the crops, cut and fetch the firewood, prepare the food, build the houses, and rear the children." Men sometimes helped raise the houses and clear the fields, but they were mainly concerned with hunting and warfare.

The villages were inhabited only from spring until fall, while the women tended the fields. During the winter months, the villagers journeyed in small groups to the west, where they hunted buffalo and lived in tipis. On the Plains or off, leadership of the community was in the hands of the principal warriors, who elected a chief and subchief to govern with the warriors' advice and consent. Power sometimes passed from father to son, but only if the younger man proved deserving of the honor.

The greater part of the fighting involved small parties led by warriors who were seeking glory or vengeance. An untried warrior might have difficulty raising a war party, but a distinguished one need only invite men to his lodge and ask them to join him in claiming scalps, captives, and booty from the enemy. A warrior's successes were often depicted symbolically on his tipi cover—and recounted on winter evenings, when Wichita warriors passed the time by

Above, mounted Wichitas follow a woman serving as their ceremonial leader during the Green Corn Dance, a celebration that was held when the corn first ripened. Ceremonial leaders like the couple at left carried ears of corn, among other sacred objects. According to Wichita lore, corn was given by the spirits to First Man and First Woman at the beginning of the world.

trading stories of past heroics. Occasionally a man might yield to the temptation to exaggerate his feats. But in a close society such as that of the Wichita, falsifiers were quickly exposed.

During the period that a man was off at war, his wife had her own role to play. She was expected to dress in rags and to shun all festivity; to do otherwise was to invite evil. At dawn, beneath the morning star that Wichitas revered as the spirit of the first human created, she would bathe in the nearest stream and pray to a merciful power called Woman Forever in the Water, asking for the strength to remain faithful. If the wife behaved properly and the warrior returned in triumph, her husband's female relatives responded by dressing her in new finery. There followed days of rejoicing with feasts and victory dances. If a warrior brought back an enemy scalp, his mother and mother-in-law would celebrate by joyfully giving away many of their possessions.

For all their determination, the Wichita were a relatively small tribe and faced powerful opposition. Beginning in the late 1600s, they started drifting southward, first into Oklahoma and later into Texas. The principal cause of this migration was pressure from the more populous Osage, who were pushing into the area from the east. Unlike the Wichita and Hasinai, the Osage were Siouan speakers, who themselves had been displaced from their forest homeland along the Ohio River by well-armed Iroquois raiders as well as by tribes the advancing Iroquois had uprooted.

The Osage found this new country much to their liking. They first built villages along the fertile, game-rich banks of the Osage River in western Missouri and soon expanded southward and westward into Kansas, Oklahoma, and Arkansas. Skilled farmers, avid hunters, and redoubtable warriors, they would dominate the eastern fringe of the southern Plains well into the 18th century. Among their neighbors and rivals were another former Ohio Valley tribe that had been displaced by the Iroquois, the Siouan-speaking Quapaw, who settled around the confluence of the Arkansas and Mississippi Rivers, where they played an important role in trade.

In appearance, the Osage were somewhat taller and lighter skinned than the Caddoan speakers. Otherwise they looked much the same, dressing in tanned hides and favoring a scalp-lock hair style for men and elaborate tattoos for both sexes. A successful warrior not only inscribed marks of honor on his chest and shoulders but often had his wife and daughters tattooed as a reflection of his glory—to the point where some women were covered with symbols from the neck down. Both men and women also painted their bodies; women each day ran a streak of red down the part in their hair to denote the path of the sun.

The Osage congregated in villages of up to 1,000 people. Extended families of from 10 to 15 kinspeople lived in rectangular houses reminiscent of their eastern past—20 feet wide and 40 or more feet long. The wooden frame was covered originally with mats of woven marsh grass and later by buffalo hides as well.

Dwellings were grouped according to clan, and the various clans were divided into two complements—the Tsi-zhu, representing the sky and peace; and the Hon-ga, representing the earth and war (the Hon-ga were further subdivided into the earth's two components, land and water). The system afforded each clan member a larger identity within the tribe and promoted cooperation between the two sides. The Tsi-zhu clans provided food for ailing children of the Hon-ga, for example. To ensure tribal unity, people could seek mates only from the opposite complement. In this manner, every marriage reunited the tribal universe, bringing together the earth and the sky.

All things under heaven, the Osage believed, were manifestations of a supreme power called Wa-kon-da, to whom they prayed each day at dawn. "These Indians have a native religion of their own," wrote the territorial governor of Arkansas in 1820. "They appeared to be as devout in their way as any class of people."

Within each clan, the men aspired to seven degrees of ceremonial knowledge that could be obtained only through much effort and expense. The first degree of the Buffalo Bull People Clan, for example, required the candidate to secure the pelts of a lynx, a gray fox, a cougar, a black bear, a buffalo, an elk, and a white-tailed deer. Once he had collected the pelts, the candidate was expected to provide gifts and food to the participants during a three-day ceremony.

Those members of the tribe who acquired all seven degrees were known as Little Old Men and formed a council that wielded secular as well as religious power. They prepared the clans for war by conducting long ceremonies that helped prevent warriors from acting impulsively (although in emergencies, war parties sometimes hurried off unceremoniously). Warriors gained status through brave deeds that were ranked in 13 grades, the highest being valor while defending the village and its womenfolk. Warriors who achieved all 13 were invited by the Little Old Men to recite their accomplishments before the assembled tribe.

Like the Iroquois and some other assertive tribes, the Osage occasionally mounted raids in order to atone for the loss of a loved one, whether or not that person had died at the hands of the enemy. According to legend, this custom originated when a leading member of the tribe was in mourning. Having smeared his face with mud and retired to fast and pray to Wa-kon-da, he was visited by the spirit of his dead relative, who complained that the spirit land was lonely and asked his living kinsman to kill someone to accompany him into the next world. In response to the plea, the kinsman mounted a raid, claimed the life of an enemy, and brought his scalp to the dead relative's grave.

Such mourning raids often provoked retaliation, which led in turn to calls for vengeance and embroiled the Osage in chronic conflict. One factor that helped keep the embattled tribe sturdy and numerous was the Osage habit of adopting captives, particularly women and children. The Osage also had rituals to promote peace, including the Calumet Dance, during which the rival parties smoked pipes and traded gifts.

The leadership of the village rested with two hereditary chiefs, one from the Tsi-zhu and one from the Hon-ga, who ruled with the advice and consent of the Little Old Men. Equal in authority, the chiefs served as moderators and magistrates and had the power to execute troublemakers, if deemed necessary. As befitted the nature of his group, the Hon-ga chief played a prominent role in time of war, while the Tsi-zhu chief was concerned mainly with peaceful activities. Visitors always stayed in the Tsi-zhu chief's lodge and conducted their business through him.

Shown here are weapons that were wielded by Osage warriors, including a bow (top); a foot-long bone dagger (right) carved from the snout of a paddlefish; and an iron-bladed hatchet (above), whose adornments include brass bells and a golden eagle tail feather, which was trimmed in a zigzag pattern to represent lightning and clipped at the end to signify the taking of an enemy head.

Osage men pictured in warrior's garb about 1900 display such traditional adornments as tattoos and roaches made of tufted deer hair along with contemporary items, including a Colt revolver. In earlier times, the powerful warrior tradition of the Osage helped them dis-place rivals such as the Wichita and push out onto the eastern edge of the Plains.

The Osage spent winters in small camps spread out along the edge of the forest, where firewood was easier to come by and game was more plentiful. With the coming of spring, they returned to their main villages to clear the fields of last year's debris and to plant the corn, squash, beans, and other crops that supplied up to three-fourths of their diet. By late May, the gardens were well established, and villagers set out for the Plains, traveling light and leaving behind the infirm and elderly members of the group, who cared for themselves as best they could. On the trail as in the villages, the two chiefs were in charge, both sharing equal responsibility for the success and safety of the party. With five assistants each, they chose camping places, sent out scouts to find the buffalo, planned the hunt, and maintained discipline throughout.

By late July, the Osage were ready to return to their villages. The packs were heavy with hides and preserved meat. Once they were back home, the people harvested their crops, gathered wild fruits and nuts, and stalked local game. The harvest was in by late September, at which time the Osage departed again for the Plains to pursue the buffalo when they were plump from browse and growing thick winter coats. Returning home at year's end with fresh bounty, the Osage rested briefly in their villages before dividing into extended family groups and dispersing for the winter.

In their periodic ventures west onto the short-grass buffalo range, all the village-dwelling tribes from the east had to reckon with bands of free-roaming hunter-gatherers, who deeply resented such intrusions. Those westerners were less cohesive than the encroaching easterners. But they were more than willing to fight.

Among the original occupants of the short-grass country were the Tonkawa, who spoke a unique language, distinct from Caddoan, and ranged in small bands across the expanse known today as the Edwards Plateau, in south-central Texas. They tended to be tall and slender, wore buckskins like other Plains dwellers, and lived in small, squat tipis or lean-tos made of brush that were easily constructed and as easily abandoned. They practiced no agriculture, but harvested wild growth assiduously. The women collected all manner of herbs, roots, seeds, and buds, including the fruit of the prickly pear cactus. The men were constantly on the chase, armed with lances, bows, and arrows. They dipped their stone arrowheads in the juice of the mistletoe leaf, which was thought to make the missiles deadlier. The weapons were lethal enough in the hands of agile men who could sneak to within easy range of a grazing deer or buffalo.

When big game was hard to come by, they settled for rabbits, rattlesnakes, and any palatable carrion they found. Women dried the surplus meat, often pounding it up with pecan meal to form pemmican, which they stuffed into animal intestines.

Each Tonkawa band followed a chief who was chosen for his leadership qualities. He might double as the war leader, but respected men were free to mount their own raiding parties, of which there were many. In time, conflict and other adversity reduced the Tonkawa in number. By 1800 the dwindling bands had coalesced into a single tribal unit of fewer than 1,000 people. Yet the Tonkawa retained a fearsome reputation, which stemmed in part from reports that they ate the flesh of their enemies in ritual fashion. An Anglo-Texan named John Jenkins told of

COMANCHE WOMAN

seeing some Tonkawas dismember the body of a Wichita warrior, then cook the hands and feet along with some beef. The Tonkawas explained to Jenkins that they meant to hold a dance and feed the victim's flesh to their women, "believing that this would make them bring forth brave men who would hate their enemies and be able to endure hardness and face dangers." Acts of cannibalism were also reported in earlier times among various Caddo groups living to the east of the Tonkawa. Whatever form those grim ceremonies took, the participants had the same purpose in mind—to absorb the enemy's spirit power.

For all their bitter conflict with intruders like the Hasinai and the Wichita, the Tonkawa's keenest traditional foes lived on the open grasslands as they did—the Apache, a strong, canny people of Athapaskan stock who had filtered southward from Canada. Ultimately most of them would be ousted by the Comanche and migrate south toward the Rio Grande or westward as far as Arizona. When Spaniards first encountered them in the 1500s, however, they roamed freely over the short-grass buffalo range, dominating an area of perhaps 250,000 square miles, extending from central Texas up through western Oklahoma and Kansas and out across eastern Colorado and New Mexico.

Coming upon the Apaches near the Arkansas River in 1601, the Spanish captain Juan de Oñate described a bustling encampment of 5,000 Indians—an estimate that was almost certainly inflated. Another Spaniard, Father Alonso de Benavides, insisted in 1630 that the "huge Apache nation

The portraits shown here and on the following pages reflect the diverse tribal population of the southern Plains, ranging from farming and foraging groups in the east, such as the Caddoan-speaking Hasinai and Wichita and the Siouan-speaking Osage and Quapaw, to hunter-gatherers in the west like the Tonkawa, Apache, Comanche, and Kiowa.

BAR-ZIN-DEBAR, CADDO

CHIEF TA-HA, KIOWA APACHE

alone has more people than all the nations of New Spain." In truth, a reliable estimate of the Apache population was next to impossible, for they were divided into more than 20 bands, of which the Lipans of west Texas and environs and the Jicarillas up along the New Mexico-Colorado border were among the biggest and strongest. As a rule, Apache bands kept to themselves, for the scant resources of their country did not permit groups to come together for long.

Unlike the Tonkawa, the Apache practiced agriculture on a limited basis in those areas where conditions permitted it, planting corn, squash, beans, and pumpkins. They also harvested wild foods, notably the century plant and other agaves that flourished in the drier parts of the region. The slow-maturing century plants, up to 30 feet tall, provided Apaches with tasty, nourishing food from flowers and bulbs as well as the tough leaf fiber they used for basketry and sandals.

When planting and harvesting, the tribespeople led a relatively settled village life. Some bands dwelt in dome-shaped, brush-covered huts later known as wickiups; others, notably the Lipans and Jicarillas, favored hide tipis, which they decorated with distinctive red and white designs. Yet most of the year, from fall through spring, they pursued buffalo, camping in small groups unobtrusively near the animals, claiming healthy bison and culling the crippled and the dead as well. Rarely did a family group take more than the few each week necessary to satisfy their immediate needs. When their prey moved on, the Apaches followed, quickly packing their

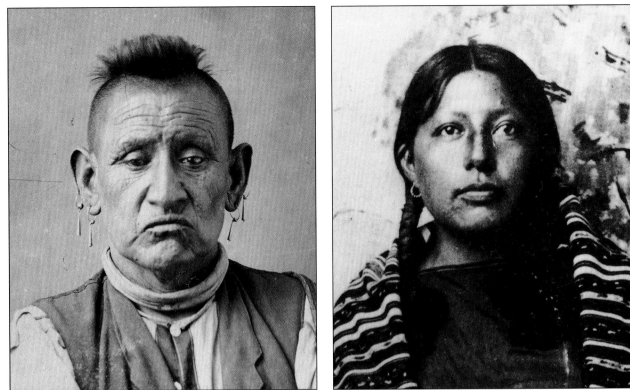

JOHN LITTLE SQUIRREL, OSAGE   KIOWA WOMAN

tipis and few belongings onto travois hauled by droves of shaggy dogs.

All Apaches were expert archers. The Lipans fashioned their bows from seasoned mountain mulberry and strung them with split and twisted bison or deer sinew; arrows were of hardwood, feathered and tipped with flint. It was essential to keep everything dry; a warped arrow was useless, and a damp bowstring had little snap. When all was right, a strong hunter could drive an arrow clear through a buffalo's hefty midriff. In the late 1600s, an admiring European observer remarked that Apaches killed buffalo "at the first shot with the greatest skill, while ambushed in brush blinds made at the watering spots."

A successful hunter immediately butchered his prize and usually ate the liver raw while it was still warm. The flesh and brains of a buffalo head were also considered delicacies and were roasted in pits, along with the large bones, from which the nutritious marrow was extracted. Fetal calves were savored for their tenderness. Blood went into puddings and stews; lungs, hearts, and tripe were boiled with vegetables; grilled udders, with or without milk, were much favored. Between kills and their attendant feasts, people made do with their pemmican.

Buffalo products of all sorts figured prominently in the lively trade Apaches carried on with the Pueblo Indians to their west. In 1598 the Spanish official Vicente de Salvidar Mendoza wrote that he had recently encountered Apaches, or "vaqueros," as he called them, "coming from trading with the Picuries and Taos, populous pueblos of this New Mexico,

CHIEF GRANT RICHARDS, TONKAWA

CHIEF ESADOWA, WICHITA

where they sell meat, hides, tallow suet, and salt in exchange for cotton blankets, pottery, maize, and some small green stones which they use." Those "small green stones" were probably turquoise, prized by Apaches for ornamental purposes.

As the Pueblos came under increasing Spanish domination, Apaches alternated trading with raiding. It may always have been so, for Apaches would readily take what they wanted when that seemed easier than bartering for it. Although they greeted the first Spanish explorers peacefully, relations soon deteriorated to the point where in 1601, Oñate's 70 or so soldiers waged a hot fight against what his aide claimed were 1,500 Apaches, who arranged themselves in a semicircle and "fought with great courage." The Spaniards reportedly scattered the Apaches with blasts from their guns, killing a number of Indians and capturing some women and boys at a cost of 30 men wounded.

If the Apaches had in fact fought a set battle with masses of men, it would have been highly uncharacteristic. Like most southern Plains warriors, Apaches typically fought in small parties led by any man who was respected enough to attract followers. The attack usually came at night or just before dawn and depended for success on surprise. If the enemy happened to be alert and put up effective resistance, the raiders customarily retreated to try again another day, for they could ill afford to suffer many losses. Victory brought booty, scalps, and captives, whom the Apaches either tortured to death upon their return to camp or adopted into the tribe.

AUGUSTIN VIGIL, JICARILLA APACHE   TALL CHIEF, QUAPAW

Youngsters and women were most commonly adopted—although any captive might be spared on a whim or for displaying some winning quality. The Lipans staged a harrowing ceremony upon returning to camp in which a male captive, unknowing of his fate, was whipped by an elderly woman until she grew arm-weary, after which he was compelled to run a gantlet and endure repeated blows with whips and clubs. Then the old woman would take the captive's head in her lap and draw a knife back and forth across his throat, barely touching the skin. This would continue at her pleasure, the captive never knowing when pantomime might give way to awful reality. At last the woman would motion the captive to rise and come to her tipi, where she would feed him and offer him rest. Come morning, he would be bathed, dressed, and painted as a Lipan. The old woman would pierce his ears with a thorn. He would receive a pair of handsome earrings—and then, at last, he would become the son of the warrior who had captured him, with all the rights and duties of a Lipan.

By such means, the Apache sought to enhance their numbers and vitality in the tumultuous period that followed their first contact with the Spaniards. The coming of Europeans was both a challenge and an opportunity, for it exposed the tribes of the southern Plains to wondrous new sources of power—horses and guns. Of the two, horses were more readily acquired by the Indians and had a greater impact. Spanish traders withheld guns from Indians, and warriors who managed to obtain firearms in

LONE TIPI, COMANCHE

other ways—through raids or through trade with the French to the east—found them of limited use. The muskets of the day were heavy and unreliable. Worse, they were so cumbersome to load that in the time it took a warrior to get off a single shot, he could fire as many as a dozen arrows. Moreover, the Indians had neither gunsmiths nor ammunition of their own. Firearms were still sought after, however, for Indians could use them to shock and intimidate their tribal competitors. And gradually the guns Indians obtained became handier and more accurate.

The horse, by contrast, brought swift and over-whelming changes. Although small by European stand-ards, the Spanish pony—descended from the Arabian stock of the Moors—was ideally suited to the semiarid Plains, being wiry, fleet, and hardy. Indians called it Mystery Dog or Big Dog, because their only experience with domestica-tion involved the canines they used as beasts of burden. The Mystery Dog was vastly superior in that role. It ate grass, not precious meat, and could bear the weight of a man on its back. Once it became established on the Plains, nothing was ever quite the same.

From an arduous, chancy enterprise afoot, the buffalo hunt became more efficient and rewarding. An expert hunter astride a swift, nimble buf-falo runner could cut out and slay five or six of the beasts in a single pass along the flank of a stampeding herd; over several days, this same hunter might be able to feed an entire village. When the buffalo moved on, it was now easy to follow along, for horses were far better than dogs at hauling travois piled high with tipi covers, belongings, buffalo meat—and passen-gers too young or feeble to mount up themselves.

Here as on the northern Plains, more meat meant less reliance on the vagaries of agriculture. Even the eastern village dwellers tended to em-brace a more nomadic lifestyle. Everywhere, populations expanded, as families grew larger, healthier, wealthier, and more secure. Tipis grew in size from five or six feet in height with a cover weighing about 60 pounds—the most a dog could carry—to 12 or 15 feet in height, with a cov-er that might require 20 buffalo skins and weigh as much as 250 pounds. Along with greater mobility came an acceleration of trade among the tribes. And since less effort was required to supply food, the menfolk had more time to devote to warfare and more incentive to raid for the horses

Three mounted Jicarilla Apache women keep company amid a herd of horses in New Mexico. After acquiring the horse from Spaniards in the 17th century, Apaches became equine traders and raiders, helping to spread the horse across the southern Plains and beyond.

that brought them prosperity and prestige. Life changed for the women as well. Wives were hard pressed to keep up with the demands of processing all the meat and skins their men brought home. A good hunter might take a second wife, often one of the younger sisters of his first wife, to help with the chores. A particularly successful hunter might eventually have several wives laboring in his household.

To a greater or lesser degree, all tribes of the southern Plains found their existence transformed by the horse. But the Apache were the first to acquire the animals in significant numbers, and they helped disseminate horses across the region. Through trading or raiding, they began to obtain mounts from the Spanish-dominated Pueblos in the mid-1600s.

In 1680 the Pueblo Indians rose up against the Spaniards, killing a great many of them and forcing the survivors to flee southward. Even though Spanish colonists returned to the upper Rio Grande in force 12 years later, the Pueblo Revolt emptied many ranches in New Mexico. The Apache profited by making off with hundreds if not thousands of horses. They traded some of them to the Wichita and Osage. The others they tried to retain, but with some difficulty. Ordinarily, the adopted captive children in an Apache band had the job of caring for the horses—all except the prized buffalo runners, which were picketed by the owner's tent. But now there were too many horses for the keepers to control, and many ran wild.

For a year or two, Apaches were able to restore their herds from the stock that remained on the Spanish pastures in New Mexico. But they soon looked southward to Mexico. In 1686 a strong war party crossed the Rio Grande below El Paso and rode far up the Rio Conchos to raid the old, well-established Spanish ranches there. They stole several hundred horses, thus setting a pattern of raids into Mexico that would continue in one form or another for the next two centuries.

The Apache cast eager eyes to the north and east as well. Formidable raiding parties of up to 100 warriors followed respected leaders on journeys of several hundred miles. Both the Wichita and Osage felt their sting. Some of the captives claimed by the Apache were sold to the Spaniards as slaves, either in the New Mexico colonies that were reconstituted after the Pueblo Revolt, or in Mexico itself. Still, the slave trade was of secondary importance for the Apache. They counted their real wealth in buffalo and in horses, not in humans.

The period of Apache ascendancy as horsemen on the southern Plains was brief, lasting only from about 1680 until the early 1700s. By then other tribes had learned the inestimable value of the animal and were gathering substantial herds. And that did not bode well for the Apache.

To the east of the Apachería—as the Spaniards referred to the Apache homeland—the Osage also benefited from the introduction of the horse. Although they never experienced a windfall of horses such as the Apache enjoyed, they were able to secure mounts slowly and steadily, and by the 1690s they had collected substantial herds. Within the highly stratified Osage society, horses opened fresh opportunities for advancement. Men who acquired horses by means of trading or raiding prospered as buffalo hunters and could then use their bounty to acquire even more mounts. A young man who succeeded in this manner could expect to marry well, for his value as a husband was gauged by the number of horses he bestowed on the family of his would-be bride. The animal was also favored as a gift to the tribe's chiefs and priests.

Some tensions were stirred up among the Osage by the introduction of the horse and this new way of separating the haves from the have-nots. By and large, however, they made the most of the opportunity and welcomed the changes in their way of life. They claimed more buffalo over a wider range and with greater ease than they could ever have imagined. In war, they grew stronger than before, raiding tribes to the south and dealing occasional setbacks to the redoubtable Apache to the west.

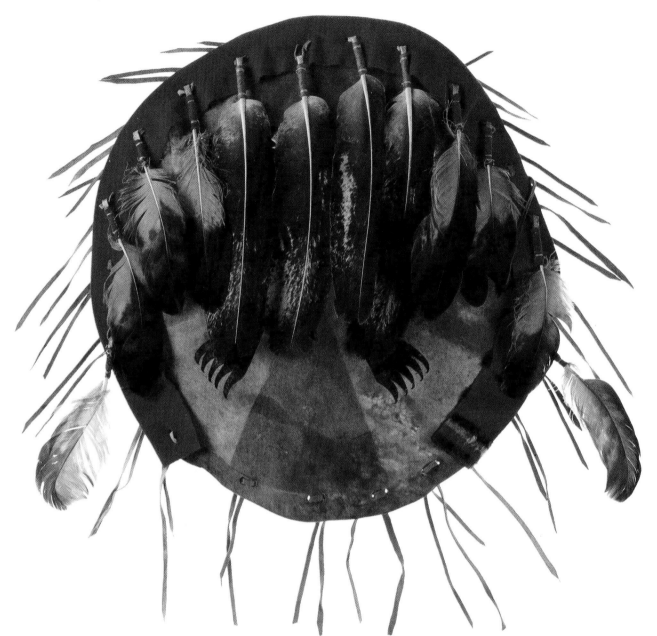

One goal of the Osage was to keep other groups from dealing with venturesome French traders, who were offering Indians guns and metal implements in exchange for furs and horses. The Osage wanted to monopolize that trade, and they lashed out repeatedly at rivals such as the Wichita. The Osage remained formidable in their prairie homeland, but they would soon encounter fresh opposition during their journeys westward onto the open grasslands—newcomers who would ultimately outdo even the Apache as hunter-warriors and take control of the country.

The arrival of a powerful new group on the southern Plains was heralded in the year 1705, when a party of Ute Indians from Colorado appeared with members of a strange tribe at the Spanish trading post in the New Mexi-

This rawhide shield, crafted by a tribal artist on the southern Plains in the early 1900s, is trimmed with eagle feathers and red felt and decorated with black claws resembling those of a bear. Although produced for trade, it evokes the medicine shields that warriors of the region carried for physical and spiritual protection.

can pueblo of Taos, situated near the western fringe of the grasslands and long a favorite destination of Plains traders and raiders. The strangers were short and heavyset. To the Spaniards, their language sounded different from that of the Utes. But the Utes, with whom the Pueblos could converse, explained that their companions were members of a distantly related tribe. For now, the strangers appeared to be on good terms with the Utes, but there may have been trouble between the two groups in the past, for the Utes called them *koh-mahts*, or "enemies." The Spaniards wrote down the name as *komantcia*, thus entering the word *Comanche* into the lexicon of the Plains.

Both Utes and Comanches were at ease on horseback, but Comanches soon gained a reputation as superior riders. More than one observer in the years to come would remark on the transformation that occurred when the seemingly ungainly Comanches mounted up. As the 19th-century American artist and chronicler George Catlin put it, the Comanches astride their horses "seem at once metamorphosed and surprise the spectator with the ease and elegance of their movements." At Taos the mission of the Utes and Comanches was to trade for more horses. The Spaniards were wary of the strangers and refused—whereupon the Indians boldly stole a few animals and galloped away onto the Plains.

The Comanche may indeed have been distantly related to the Ute, for both were members of the large Uto-Aztecan language family. The Co-

A warrior unleashes an arrow while hanging over the side of his mount for protection in this sketch by George Catlin showing some of the maneuvers Comanche horsemen practiced assiduously before entering battle.

manche belonged to a distinct branch of that family, however. They spoke a dialect akin to that of the Shoshone who lived north of the Ute along the western flank of the Rocky Mountains. When and why the Comanche split off from the mountain-dwelling Shoshone is not known precisely. According to one tribal legend, the son of a chief was killed by a boy from another band during a rough-and-tumble game; the dead boy's family wanted revenge, but decided to leave the main band rather than spill the blood of their kin. According to a second legend, the dispute was over the rights to a bear taken in a joint hunt, and when neither side could agree to share the carcass, one group went north and the other south.

Whatever spurred the migration, there was probably no great exodus of Shoshones from the mountains to the southern Plains. It seems that in the late 1600s, small hunting groups came down out of the hills to pursue buffalo. They were lured as well by the promise of obtaining horses, for few Shoshones had mounts at the time. One Comanche later remarked that when his ancestors came down from the north, they traveled on foot and "packed their property on their backs." Soon the migrants acquired ponies and prospered. Their success encouraged others to follow, until the former mountain dwellers were established in force on the southern Plains.

By 1700 there may have been as many as 7,000 of these Comanches scattered from New Mexico and Colorado across Texas to Oklahoma and Kansas. They called themselves Nermernuh, or Nerm, meaning simply "the people." Over time, as Comanche bands within a given area came together periodically to hunt or to socialize, they coalesced into larger groups, which became known as divisions. Those divisions remained on good terms with one another. But they acknowledged no central authority and retained their distinct identities—even as the Comanche as a whole swept aside the Apache and other native rivals during the course of the 18th century and emerged as lords of the southern Plains.

Imbued with the power of the animal that sustained the tribe, Comanche buffalo-horn headdresses like the one worn by the warrior opposite proclaimed the bravery and accomplishment of fighting men. The example below is wrapped in hide embroidered with beadwork.

Like the Shoshones they left behind in the mountains, the Comanche divisions were known by the name of a particular food they savored or by some other salient trait. Among the largest and strongest of the groups by the late 18th century were the Penateka, or Honey Eaters, so called for the nectar they gathered from combs in the woods of their Texas homeland near the Edwards Plateau. They were closest to the white settlements in south Texas, which they raided assiduously. North of the Penateka, between the Colorado and Red Rivers, lived the Nokoni, or Wanderers, who roamed more freely than the other divisions. Above the Nokoni dwelt the seven or eight bands of the Kotsoteka, or Buffalo Eaters, whose domain was home to some of the greatest concentrations of bison. Still farther north were the Yamparika, or Root Eaters. They were the last group to leave the mountains and subsisted in large part on buffalo like the others, but they retained the old Shoshone custom of unearthing edible roots. The westernmost Comanches were the Quahada, or Antelope People, who split off from the Kotsoteka perhaps as late as 1800 and found a new home on the high plains of west Texas and New Mexico, where herds of antelope supplemented the supply of bison.

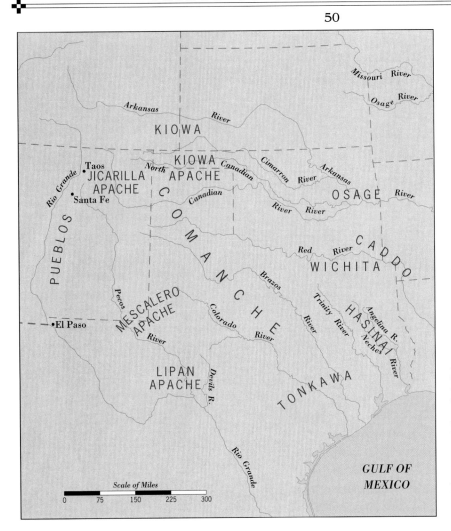

By the late 18th century, the tribal makeup of the southern Plains had changed significantly. In the early 1700s, Comanches swept down from the north and seized control of the open grasslands from the Apache, who ended up in arid country to the south and west. Later, Kiowas and Kiowa Apaches established themselves in and around the Texas Panhandle, where they made peace with Comanches. To the east, the Osage expanded from southwestern Missouri into neighboring parts of Arkansas, Kansas, and Oklahoma—which in turn put pressure on the Wichita to migrate southward.

Overall, the Comanchería, as the Spaniards called Comanche country, stretched across 240,000 square miles. By the mid-1700s, the population had grown to perhaps 20,000, making the Comanche the most populous and powerful group on the southern Plains. For that they had the horse to thank—the animal that gave them mobility as hunters and raiders. Indeed, one of the chief motivations for Comanche raiding parties was to obtain more horses. Their main targets were the Spanish settlements in New Mexico and Texas, but they did not overlook herds amassed by rival tribes. Both Indians and whites would long marvel at their skill in making off with horses. As Colonel Richard Dodge of the U.S. Cavalry observed in the 1800s, "For crawling into a camp, cutting hopples and lariat ropes, and getting off undiscovered with the animals, they are unsurpassed and unsurpassable." It was said that a Comanche could sneak up to a group of sleeping men, cut loose the prized horses roped to their wrists, and slip away with the animals without rousing a soul.

Comanches were equally skilled at capturing the wild mustangs that ranged the Plains. Employing tactics similar to those used to trap buffalo, men would build large corrals with wide, fan-shaped mouths near water holes. They would then surround a herd of wild horses and drive them into the corral, where the ponies were lassoed—a technique picked up from the Spaniards. Alternatively, men would wait in ambush near a water hole for a herd of thirsty wild horses to approach. Once the horses drank their fill, the Comanches would chase after the animals and rope them. Winter was a good time to catch horses, for at that season, they were often weak from cold and hunger.

Unlike many other Plains tribes, the Comanche excelled as horse breeders as well, showing a preference for the vividly marked pintos. They took good care of the mares and gelded all but the finest stallions in order to improve bloodlines. In contrast to the Apache, who preferred to fight on foot, the Comanche waged war avidly from horseback. Their mounts had to be steady enough to withstand the strain of battle and sensitive enough to respond to pressure from a rider's knees or shifting weight while his hands were busy with weapons. A favorite Comanche tactic was to hang down along the flank of the horse, supported only by one heel over the animal's back and a shoulder strap woven into the mane; from that position, a warrior with his short, four-foot-long bow could loose a stream of arrows from under the horse's neck while remaining shielded by its body. All the while, the horse would gallop steadily ahead. A buffalo horse needed the courage and stamina to stay with a stampeding herd—and the agility to dodge the thrust of a wounded bull. Such runners were trained to close on a fleeing animal, then veer away without any command save the twang of the bow.

Even with selective breeding, only a few horses displayed such noble qualities. Yet the Comanche had huge herds to choose from. One band of 2,000 members was known to have 15,000 horses, plus 400 mules to help as pack animals. A prominent chief among the Sioux would be happy with 50 head to call his own, while a Comanche family might claim five times as many and a chief might possess even more.

When they were not raiding for horses, the Comanche exercised their skills as cunning horse traders. Many other tribes of the region obtained their mounts from the Comanche. Their tongue in fact became the language of trade across the area, as Comanches swapped horses and buffalo hides for tobacco, cloth, and as time went on, all manner of metal items, from knives and arrowheads to pots and other household utensils—which they secured either directly from Europeans or from tribes dealing with them. Among the trade items favored by Comanche men were multiple wristbands of copper wire, which served both as ornaments and as protection against the slap of the bowstring.

Encamped near the Canadian River in 1869, a band of Kiowas finds shelter beneath a stand of cottonwood trees, which flourished along waterways throughout the southern Plains. Unlike the settled Hasinai and Wichita with their grass lodges, the roving Kiowa and Comanche lived in buffalo-hide tipis.

In their horse-focused culture, all Comanches rode—men, women, children, and even infants. At the age of five, a boy might own his first horse, practicing daily like an athlete until he became expert at riding either bareback or in the light saddle that the Indians adapted from the Spaniards. Youths learned to pick up objects from the ground at full speed and, by the time they were men, could rescue a dismounted warrior by swinging him up behind them on the horse. If the warrior was injured, two riders would approach in tandem and each grasp an arm to lift the man onto one of the horses. No Comanche ever left behind a comrade if he could possibly avoid it.

Girls also learned to ride at an early age—and to perform the many arduous chores that fell to the Plains woman. The wife of a good buffalo hunter had so much work to do processing the carcasses that he brought home and performing her other duties that she seldom resented sharing her lodge with a second wife, particularly if that woman was her sister. A woman's routine was also eased by the help she received from her parents, siblings, and other kin in raising the children.

There were some hardships she had to bear alone, however. The long days that pregnant women spent on horseback resulted in many miscarriages, often with grave complications for the mother. And the marriages were not always happy ones. Here as elsewhere in the region, a husband was chosen for his skills as a provider, measured in the number of horses he offered the bride's family. A suitor frequently had to wait until he was 25 or 30 years old before he could make a bid large enough to win over a young woman's family. The bride, by contrast, was usually in her mid-teens, and she had to set aside any fondness she felt for youths her own age for an alliance with an older man she knew only by reputation. Under the circumstances, it was not surprising that young women sometimes ran off with other suitors or committed adultery. Occasionally an offended husband punished the unfaithful wife by cutting off her nose or otherwise mutilating her.

Like the men, Comanche women were fond of tattooing and painting their bodies. They chopped their hair short, however, in contrast to the men, who allowed theirs to grow long and did it up in braids glistening with bear grease and adorned with feathers, beads, bits of silver, and other charms. When they made war, many Comanches donned a heavy headdress fashioned from the scalp of a buffalo bull, with the horns projecting from the top. A troop of horned Comanches, their faces painted carmine red, racing to the attack, was a sight not soon forgotten by their enemies.

Every Comanche band had its war chief, whose directions were heeded by all those volunteering for the fight. Any warrior who disagreed with the chief was free to leave the band, and the chief's power of suggestion lasted only until the group returned to camp. Similar limits were imposed on the Comanche band's other authority figure, the peace chief, who was usually an older man respected for his wisdom and generosity. His role was to offer advice and to mediate disputes.

Some esteemed chiefs exercised great and enduring influence. But none could act without consulting the band council, to which every adult male belonged. The council decided when the band should move camp and when it should wage war, which tribes could be trusted as allies or trading partners and which should be shunned. The band looked to the council for care of the elderly and the weak. No decisions were taken unless everyone agreed. If consensus could not be achieved, a decision often was postponed. Once agreement was reached, however, everyone had to either abide by it or leave the band.

The respect that members of each band showed one another was mirrored by the consideration they demonstrated for Comanches elsewhere. Whatever band or division they belonged to, Comanches honored the ties that made them one people. They were linked not only by language and custom but also by spiritual traditions. As befitted their informal and democratic ways, they had no priestly hierarchy and observed few rituals as a group. But they were fervent in their pursuit of the sacred power they called *puha,* or "medicine."

Young Comanches went off alone on vision quests at puberty and sought blessings from a spirit that frequently took the form of an animal. Those seekers fortunate enough to be visited by the eagle spirit, for example, obtained potent medicine. But every supernatural gift brought with it strict taboos. A hunter blessed by the eagle could not allow anyone to pass behind him while he ate. If he violated the taboo, he risked being harmed by his own medicine. There were other sources of danger in the Comanche spirit world, including the ghosts that haunted lonely places at night—said to be the restless spirits of enemies who had been scalped or mutilated—and monsters such as Cannibal Owl, who swooped down in the dark and devoured people.

Comanches needed bravery to deal with such menaces and to endure the various quests and trials that brought them power. Every hunt and every raid was a test of a man's medicine and an opportunity to enhance it. Some who distinguished themselves as hunters and warriors were

For Kiowa boys such as Little Joe, pictured above, membership in the Rabbit Society provided the training a youngster needed in order to succeed as a hunter and warrior and to advance up the tribal ladder, with its numerous degrees of distinction.

hailed as *puhakut,* or "medicine men." Not all puhakut were helpers or healers; a few used their talent maliciously and were dreaded as witches. And not all were men. Young women too appealed to the spirits and were blessed with strong medicine. It was considered dangerous for them to apply that power while they were still menstruating. But after menopause, they sometimes emerged as esteemed doctors.

Europeans who clashed repeatedly with Comanches and denounced them as warlike failed to appreciate that the power they sought could be acquired through peaceful means as well as violent ones. Contrary to their reputation as implacable foes, Comanches sometimes forged lasting alliances with former enemies, including the small but resolute tribe that helped them maintain their hold on the southern Plains: the Kiowa.

In the beginning, according to tribal legend, the Kiowa came into the world one by one, squirming through a hollow log. Unfortunately, not all of them were able to make the passage. At some point in the ordeal, a woman whose body was swollen with child got stuck in the log. No matter how hard she struggled, she could not move. From then on, no one further could enter the world. That was how the Kiowa got their name—derived from the term *kwuda,* or "coming out"—and that was why there were so few of them on earth.

The Kiowa may never have numbered more than 2,000 people. They spoke a language related to that of the Pueblo Indians and may have left the Southwest and ventured northward before the Spaniards appeared there. According to tribal tradition, they found a home up along the Wyoming-Montana border. During the 1700s, however, they turned back south under pressure from larger tribes. When they reached Kansas, they came up against the Osage to the east and the Comanche directly south, both of whom resented the appearance of another group of mounted buffalo hunters. Although few in number, the Kiowa were valiant and resourceful fighters, who threw up earthworks to defend their encampments, a tactic unfamiliar to their Indian foes.

The Osage remained lasting enemies. But the Comanche soon gained a healthy respect for the Kiowa. About 1790 the two sides made peace, and thereafter they shared hunting ranges amicably and even joined forces on raids against the Spaniards and other mutual enemies. At the time of their alliance with the Comanche, the Kiowa consisted of six bands. Each had its own chief, one of whom served as the principal leader. Among the six bands was a group of 350 or so Apaches who had split off from their original tribe. They had since embraced Kiowa customs so heartily that they were known as the Kiowa Apache.

Like their fellow Kiowas, Kiowa Apaches learned to trust Comanches, as evidenced by the story of a young Kiowa Apache who went off on a raid

Kiowa chief White Man stands at right, holding a lance and shield beside four well-armed warriors. Plains Indians often decorated their war lances with bright strips of cloth and other adornments, including fur, feathers, locks of hair, and enemy scalps.

into Mexico with some other members of his band and fell wounded with a bullet through the stomach. His companions abandoned him for dead, but a party of Comanches came across him in the night and cared for him. They salved his wound with the juice of a prickly pear, bound his stomach with fresh buckskin, and brought him back to their village on a travois. There he was adopted by the chief of the party. "I found this boy," the chief declared, "and from now on I will call him 'son.' " When the youngster recovered, he tended the chief's horses and later joined him on many raids. After a few years, the adopted son returned to the Kiowa Apache with the blessing of his Comanche father, who gave him two fast ponies as a parting gift.

The Kiowa—and by extension, the Kiowa Apache—resembled their Comanche allies in numerous ways. They hunted, fought, and feasted in similar fashion; dressed alike and dwelt in the same sort of buffalo-hide tipis; and were born, married, and buried in much the same manner. Yet in other respects, the Kiowa were quite different from the Comanche. For one thing, they were noticeably taller. Many Kiowa men approached six feet in height. Artist George Catlin wrote of one exceptional Kiowa "near seven feet in stature," who purportedly could run down and slay a buffalo on foot. What truly set the Kiowa apart, however, was not their physique but their highly elaborate social structure, which rivaled and in some ways surpassed that of the Osage.

In Kiowa society, every little boy enrolled in a kind of school called the Rabbit Society. According to legend, the society was founded by a reclusive old man who was banished for defying his fellow tribesmen. He nearly perished in the wild, but the rabbits took pity on him, gathering food for him and teaching him their language. Once he grew wise in their ways, the rabbits suggested that he return to the Kiowa and teach the boys how to become men. He did so and was celebrated by young Kiowas thereafter as Grandfather Rabbit.

All young Rabbits in the society wore a small headdress made of elk skin and feathers and attended classes taught by their elders in horse care, hunting, and warfare; on special occasions, they feasted and danced, hopping about in imitation of their namesakes. About the age of 12, the children graduated to another society, the Herders, where their instruction continued. As they grew older, they joined war parties, at first merely to tend the horses and later to fight.

At the age of 18, a boy became a man and joined one of the warrior dancing societies, which went by such names as the Horse Headdresses

These elaborate high-top boots decorated with beadwork and German silver studs were worn by Kiowa women on special occasions.

and the Black Legs. Each society had its own insignia, dances, and songs and was governed by two co-leaders and two whip bearers, who supervised the activities of members. Aside from their ceremonial functions, the societies policed communal buffalo hunts and generally maintained law and order within the band.

During the course of his life, a warrior might graduate from one society to a more prestigious one as his reputation grew. Yet only a select group of war leaders ever gained admission to the Koisenko, the Crazy Dogs or Principal Dogs, whose membership was restricted to the bravest of the brave. It was their duty to lead the most dangerous war charges and, if called upon, to lay down their lives for the good of their fellow Kiowas. When a Koisenko faced death, he chanted a song of praise to the world's eternal powers:

I live, but I will not live forever.
Mysterious moon, you only remain,
Powerful sun, you alone remain,
Wonderful earth, you remain forever.

Kiowa men were distinguished not only by the society to which they belonged but also by rank. There were four classes—the elite, who were wealthy, generous, and brave enough to be eligible for the Koisenko if they were not already members; the second best, who were men of means but had yet to accomplish much; men without property; and mere hangers-on.

Paralleling the warrior societies was a constellation of shield, or medicine, societies—among them the Eagle Shields, composed of shamans who summoned spirits; the Buffalo Shields, who cured wounds and mended broken bones; and the Owl Shields, who dealt in prophecy. Kiowa women also had their own societies. The Calf Old Women danced and feasted in an innocent manner. Not so the Bear Women, whose leader approached the tipi where a feast had been spread out and scratched at the door while growling like a grizzly.

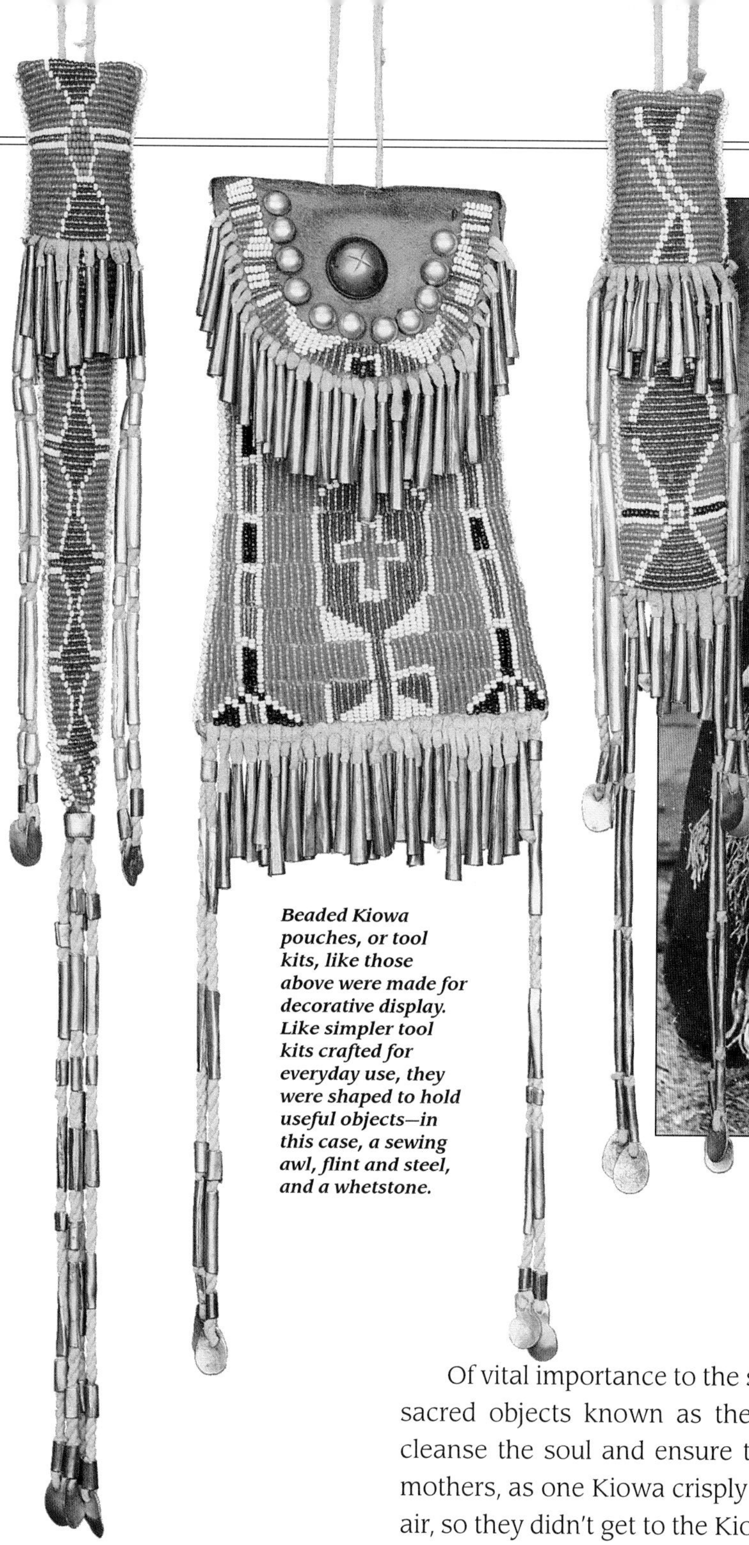

Beaded Kiowa pouches, or tool kits, like those above were made for decorative display. Like simpler tool kits crafted for everyday use, they were shaped to hold useful objects—in this case, a sewing awl, flint and steel, and a whetstone.

The daughters of Kiowa chief Big Tree exhibit some of their finest attire. The girl standing at right boasts a beaded tool kit and a buckskin dress decorated with elk's teeth. Her seated sister wears fancy high-top boots similar to those shown opposite.

Of vital importance to the spiritual life of the tribe were the bundles of sacred objects known as the Ten Grandmothers, which were said to cleanse the soul and ensure the welfare of all Kiowas. The Ten Grandmothers, as one Kiowa crisply put it, "sucked all the bad things out of the air, so they didn't get to the Kiowas. That way, as long as they take care of the Ten Grandmothers, the Kiowas are safe."

Each of the 10 bundles was entrusted to a family—often that of a chief—who guarded it devoutly. The tipis where the Grandmothers resided were believed to be sacred; Kiowas came to them to pray and offer gifts and sometimes sought sanctuary there from enemies within the tribe. Every year the Ten Grandmothers themselves were renewed. The guardians would bring them to the ceremonial tipi of a special priest. Alone, the priest would open the bundles, inspect the contents, cleanse them in a steam bath, blow purifying smoke over the objects, and then pack them up and return them to their guardians.

The Kiowa observed many rituals, but no ceremony was more important to the tribe than the Sun Dance. Celebrated in midsummer when the power of the sun was at its peak, the event brought all Kiowas together to honor the supreme force in heaven that bequeathed warmth and vitality to the earth. If properly honored, the sun would reward the Kiowa with plentiful bison, great horse herds, many fine children, protection against sickness and other evils, and success in warfare. When the six bands gathered for the event, they camped next to one another in a great circle.

The direction of the Sun Dance fell to a priest who cared for the sacred *taime,* which linked the tribe symbolically to the sun. Originally this image was fashioned from buckskin, but by the 1800s it took the form of a painted stone sculpture about two feet tall and garbed in robes of white feathers with ermine pendants. The image represented a legendary young woman who, it was said, climbed a tree to heaven and married the son of the sun, only to perish when she fell back to earth. The priest kept the taime in a rawhide pouch, which he never opened to public view except during the Sun Dance. Guarding the priest and the sacred image were men of an honored society, the Sun Dance Shields.

Great ceremony attended the construction of the huge medicine lodge amid the tribal circle, where the dance itself would take place. The warrior societies staged symbolic attacks to conquer the area. A young warrior and his wife set out in search of an albino buffalo bull, which he had to slay with a single arrow; if no albino could be found, a yearling bull would suffice. The meat would later be distributed to the Sun Dance priest and the Sun Dance Shields, while the skin would hold offerings bestowed on the sacred taime.

A small cottonwood tree was then selected to serve as the center pole for the lodge. A young captive girl was delegated to chop it down, for the spirit in the tree was powerful and Kiowas were reluctant to risk one of their own. Men and women shared in the construction of the lodge, amid much horseplay and lovemaking. When all was ready, another captive, this time a male, stepped forward to uncover the taime so that it could be elevated for all to see. If he somehow made a mistake and angered the spirits, it would be best if he was not a Kiowa.

The ceremony lasted about 10 days. Various rituals sacred to the tribe might be performed by different societies during this period, including the Gourd Dance. But the supreme observance was the Sun Dance itself. The Sun Dance priest, his four assistants, and the members of the Sun Dance Shield Society were the main performers. But anyone who hoped to be-

This wand tipped with feathers was crafted in the early 1900s to represent the taime of the Kiowa—a sacred image decorated with feathers and held aloft on a pole during the tribe's Sun Dance. The original taime, acquired from an Arapaho who married a Kiowa in the mid-1700s, was kept by the couple's descendants. A member of that family created the replica above for display on nonsacred occasions.

come a more successful warrior or hunter or to father many children might join in for as long as he felt the urge and had the stamina. The dancers' upper bodies were painted white, and they wore long white buckskin skirts overlaid with blue breechcloths. Each man faced the taime and danced in place, flexing his knees up and down to the beat of drums and the singing of women. In their teeth the dancers clenched eagle-bone whistles, and their escaping breath added to the music. The leader of the Sun Dance Shields played a special part. He would stand at the lodge entrance and stare fixedly at the sun before launching into a frenzied dance that left him exhausted.

Periodically the Sun Dance priest would pray to the taime and take up a feather fan placed near the image. Half running, half hopping, he would then cut one of the dancers out of the circle with the fan and pursue him around the arena until the dancer fell to the ground in a trance. Then it would be another man's turn, and another's, until all the dancers had fallen under the spell of the fan. Each dancer hoped to experience visions while in a trance. If such inspiration occurred, he would then call for a pipe and relate what he had seen.

When the sixth day drew to a close, the dancers each received a small medicinal potion to drink. The taime was lovingly packed away, and Kiowas sacrificed clothing—and perhaps even a horse—as a final offering to the sun. No war or hunting parties had gone out during the festivities. And the Kiowas had been severely enjoined to keep their hearts and minds clean and pure, and to speak and act kindly. Excitement or discord of any sort would destroy the power of the ritual.

Now the hunts could commence anew and war parties could go forth with fresh confidence. The leaders of the various bands would part company, most of them not to meet again until the next year. They had taken this opportunity to come together as an informal tribal council and to settle any lingering disputes that threatened tribal harmony.

At times such as these, the Kiowa were one people under the sun. And they occasionally extended that spirit of acceptance to others, most notably their allies the Comanche. However, theirs was not an environment that was conducive to harmony between peoples. The open country, and the buffalo that ranged there, knew no boundaries. The Kiowa and Comanche may have found peace with one another, but they remained deeply at odds with other tribes—as well as with the light-skinned intruders who constituted the most serious threat to their fragile hold on this alluring and unforgiving land. ❖

PAINTED TIPIS OF THE KIOWA

Sturdy, portable, and easily assembled after a long day's ride, the hide tipi provided an ideal shelter for the roving, buffalo-hunting tribes of the southern Plains. Among the Kiowa, the tipi also served an important symbolic function—as a backdrop for vibrant paintings that held profound meaning for the occupants and their neighbors. The designs were inspired by bold deeds or stirring dreams and visions that linked the tipi holder to powerful spirits and their medicine. Cherished as family heirlooms, the designs—and the medicine associated with them—passed from one generation to the next. When a tipi wore out, the design was ceremonially renewed and transferred to fresh buffalo hides, sometimes with changes that reflected recent dreams or events.

Not all Kiowas held rights to painted tipis. Fewer than one in four of the community's dwellings were so decorated at any given time. The tipi painting was a form of heraldry—a mark of distinction often claimed by chiefs, war leaders, medicine men, and their descendants. At the annual Sun Dance ceremony, when Kiowas came together and camped in a great circle around the Sun Dance lodge, the painted tipis boldly proclaimed the identity of the tribe's leading families for all to see.

In the late 19th century, as the buffalo dwindled and Kiowas were confined by troops to reservations in the Indian Territory, tribal fortunes declined and the tipi paintings faded into memory. The last great Sun Dance meeting of the Kiowa before they came under the authority of the United States was held in 1867. By 1891 only one of the painted tipis was still in use. It was then that James Mooney, an ethnographer from the Smithsonian Institution, set out to preserve a record of the painted Kiowa lodges. As shown here, he commissioned tribal members with hereditary rights to the designs to create models of the dwellings for exhibition. Dozens of tipi models were painted and preserved, enabling future generations to witness the proud tradition of Kiowa heraldry.

Above, Kiowa artist Zotom works on a model tipi for James Mooney in 1897. Zotom, a warrior who once defied the U.S. Army, received artistic encouragement while imprisoned at Fort Marion, Florida, in the 1870s. Each model that he and other Kiowas produced for the project stood about two feet high. The design at right, showing a man and a boy gripping a pipe, derived from a dream by a Kiowa Apache named Standing among Men.

Great horned fish grimace menacingly on the cover of the Underwater Monster Tipi. According to Kiowa lore, such monsters lurked in the depths, where they seized and scalped unlucky swimmers and displayed the scalps on their horns.

Ethnographer James Mooney (right) set out to re-create the camp of the Kiowa Sun Dance of 1867. His diagram (below) labels many of the 238 tipi holders by name and shows that they were grouped into six bands—five of them Kiowa and one Kiowa Apache. Although Mooney was unable to reproduce all the tipis at the Sun Dance, he exhibited many of the model lodges at an exposition in Saint Louis in 1904.

N

KINEP

BIG SHIELD

APACHE

SENAT

W

KONTÁLYUI or BLACK BOY

K´AIGWU or KIOWA PROPER

REE

C´ADO DA MEDICIN LODGE

Sun Dance Camp Circle
of the
Kiowa and Apache Indians
at
Date: Medicin Lodge Treaty 1867

James Mooney, 1896

KÓGUI

ELK

K´ATA or

S

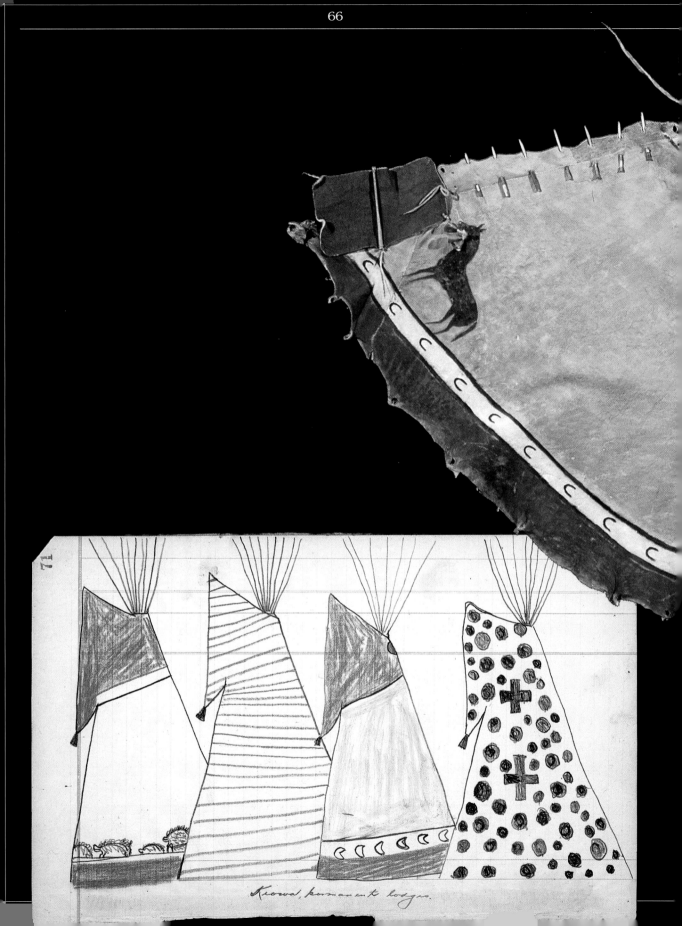

Kiowa, permanent lodges.

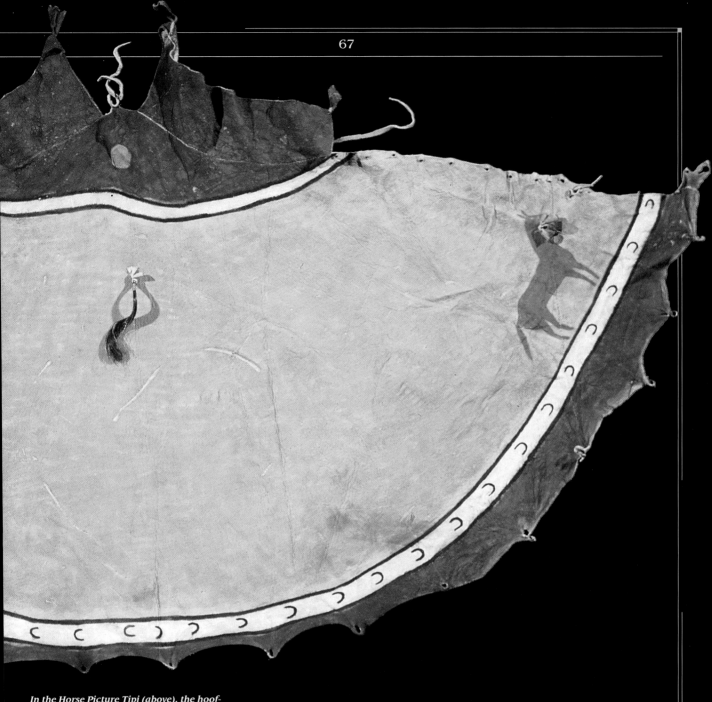

In the Horse Picture Tipi (above), the hoof-prints at bottom, fanning out in opposite directions, reveal that the horses at either end started out in the same place—and will meet again at the entryway when the model is assembled and the flaps are joined. The actual tipi, shown in the Kiowa ledger drawing at left (second from right), was once owned by a Kiowa known as Crazy Bear and was recreated from memory by his descendants.

Kiowa, permanent lodges.

The Battle Picture Tipi of Kiowa chief Dohausen, or
Little Bluff, is depicted here in three forms—in a model (top left) painted by Ohettoint, Dohausen's descend-
ant; in an anonymous ledger drawing (above, far left);
and in a photograph (left) showing Ohettoint's wife,
Mary Buffalo, on horseback in front of the actual tipi.
The last surviving Kiowa painted lodge, it was given
to Dohausen by Cheyenne chief Sleeping Bear in the
1840s after their tribes made peace. As Dohausen and
his heirs renewed the tipi, they portrayed fresh ex-
ploits, some of them involving clashes with troops.

57

At right in a mislabeled ledger drawing by an unknown Indian artist, Kiowa men and women dressed in their finest attire sing and beat drums as they approach the Leg Picture Tipi, shown at far left in the drawing and in model form below. A tipi holder honored in this way would repay the singers with a feast. The haunting image on this tipi appeared in a vision to a Kiowa known as Fair-Haired Old Man. He bequeathed the lodge to his kinsman, Brave Boy, who died in 1869.

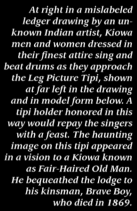

Comanche women.

ASCENT OF THE COMANCHE

Ee-shah-ko-nee, or Returning Wolf, wears two golden eagle feathers in his hair, shell earrings, and a boar-tusk pendant in this 1832 portrait of the Comanche chief by visiting artist George Catlin.

In late March 1808, a Spanish officer by the name of Francisco Amangual left San Antonio accompanied by 200 mounted men on an expedition to Santa Fe that would take them through the heart of the Comanchería. Their mission was to establish a secure route across the southern Plains—one with adequate supplies of water and friendly Indian encampments that would link the Spanish outposts in south Texas to those in New Mexico. At first Captain Amangual and his men traversed bleak terrain, with sparse grass and rocky ground that left their horses thin and lame. In early April, however, the party reached the congenial, tree-shaded banks of the San Saba River. After pausing there to recuperate, they continued toward the Texas Panhandle, where bison grazed in abundance and the Comanche reigned supreme.

Spanish relations with the tribe—once steeped in bitterness and distrust—had improved in recent times. Amangual received confirmation of that fact not long after departing the San Saba when he had a friendly encounter with Comanches led by a chief who called himself Cordero, in honor of the Spanish governor of Texas. Not all Comanches were so hospitable to outsiders, however. Amangual and his men had reason to be wary as they delved deeper into the tribe's territory.

On May 8 they approached a band of Comanches camped by a stream on a grassy plateau dotted with mesquite trees. Graced with water and abundant fuel, theirs was an enviable site, one well worth defending against encroachment. When mounted men appeared on the horizon, Comanches rode out briskly from the camp to meet them. As the Indians drew up, Amangual could see by their clothing that they were familiar with Europeans and their ways. One Comanche, the captain observed, was dressed "in the style of ancient Spain," with an outfit that included a red jacket, blue trousers, white stockings, a cocked hat, English spurs, and a cane with a silver handle. Several of his companions wore long-tailed coats or neckties, along with traditional forms of adornment that were no less striking—including bold facial paint, strings of beads and shells, and neatly braided hair that in several cases reached clear to the ground.

The ideal cavalryman of New Spain, as shown in this sketch dating from about 1803, was equipped with more than 120 pounds of weapons and accouterments, including a thick leather jacket designed to deflect arrows. Thus weighted down, the ponderous Spaniards were frequently outmaneuvered by agile Indian horsemen, who specialized in hit-and-run raids.

The appearance and manner of the Comanches suggested that they were receptive to the visitors without being cowed by them. Whatever their past dealings with Spaniards, they played the part of confident and obliging hosts. The two parties dismounted by the stream and sat down together in the shade. After partaking of refreshments, Amangual reported, they talked for nearly an hour. Although the captain had brought along an interpreter, some Comanches could now communicate directly with the Spaniards, having picked up bits of their language along with their clothing. Amangual made it clear to the leader of the band, Chief Isapampa, that he and his men were welcome to visit San Antonio and would be greeted there in friendship. Afterward, he noted with satisfaction, the Comanches returned to their lodges, "showing every sign of being pleased with our meeting together."

The Spaniards soon continued to Santa Fe. Yet this brief encounter between two proud cultures said much about both sides. The meeting not only confirmed the capacity of the supposedly relentless Comanche to come to terms with outsiders but also demonstrated how much their stature had increased in the eyes of the Spaniards since the two sides first made contact in New Mexico a century earlier. Then Spanish colonists had declined to trade with Comanches and tried to brush them off. Now they paid court to chiefs of the tribe in their remote encampments. Such concessions had not come easily, and much blood had been spilled along the way. Yet decades of hard experience had convinced the Spaniards that the Comanche were indeed lords of the Plains—that no power, Indian or European, could outdo them in their adopted setting.

From the start, relations between Comanches and Spaniards were complicated. Both groups had other rivals to consider. Spanish policy in the region was dictated initially by hostility toward the French, who traded with Indians at the eastern edge of the Plains and were suspected of inciting them against the Spaniards. Comanches, for their part, clashed frequently with Apaches, Osages, and other tribal foes. Sometimes mutual antagonism toward a particular group brought Comanches and Spaniards together for a while. But both parties were diverse and had trouble preserving accords. Comanche chiefs seldom acted in concert and had limited control over their followers, while Spanish officials in Texas and New Mexico often worked at cross purposes and sometimes ignored commitments made by their predecessors.

The Spanish outposts in Texas arose later than those in New Mexico and were never as substantial. The first missions in Texas, founded among the Hasinai in 1690, lasted only a few years. Close contact with Europeans exposed the Indians there to new and devastating diseases. When smallpox struck the Hasinai, Father Francisco Casañas assured them that it was God's "holy will." The Hasinai resisted the priests and their mysterious God and forced the Spaniards to abandon the missions in 1693. Father Casañas returned to New Mexico, where he died in a Pueblo uprising a few years later.

Concerned that the French would dominate Texas if left unchecked, Spaniards returned in 1716. New missions were planted in southeast Texas, but they fared little better than their predecessors. The Hasinai refused to leave their existing villages and settle around chapels with the priests, who were all but defenseless. "We do not have a single gun," wrote the missionaries, "while we see the French giving hundreds of arms to the Indians." Few Hasinais agreed to be baptized except on the verge of death. In the end, the chief legacy of the missions was to increase the ravages of disease among the Hasinai and neighboring Caddo. Before the century was out, European-borne diseases would afflict all the tribes in the region, but the toll was greater among settled farming peoples like the Caddo than among roving groups like the Comanche.

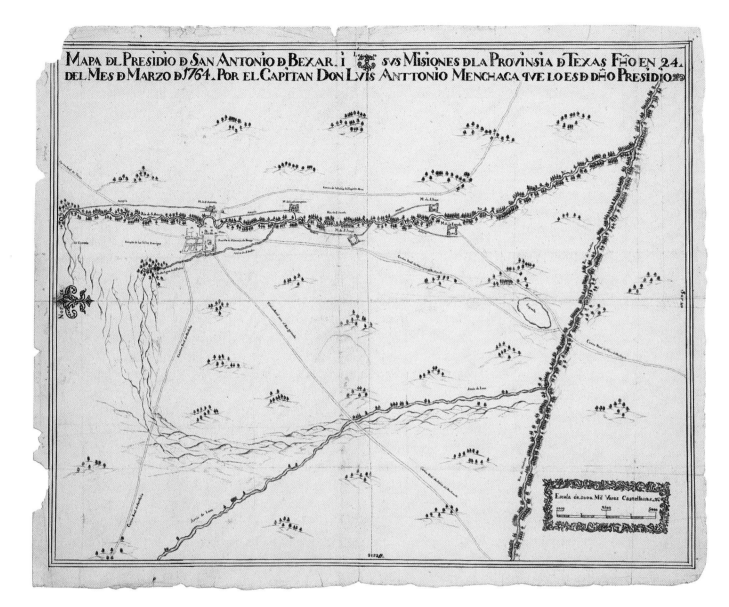

MAPA DL PRESIDIO D SAN ANTONIO D BEXAR. i svs MISIONES DLA PROVINSIA D TEXAS FÑO EN 24. DEL MES D MARZO D 1764. POR EL CAPITAN DON LVIS ANTTONIO MENCHACA QVE LO ES D DÑO PRESIDIO

An 18th-century map shows the garrison and five missions the Spaniards built along the San Antonio River between 1716 and 1731 to help New Spain expand into Texas.

Aside from the Caddo missions, several small Spanish outposts grew up elsewhere in south Texas, watched over by troops stationed at presidios. But the only colony that prospered to any extent was San Antonio. There priests gathered nearly 1,000 Indians from various tribes at a complex of missions. A garrison of troops took up residence at the local presidio, and hundreds of Spanish civilians eventually settled in the area. The main threat to the security of San Antonio in its early days came from Apaches, who were being driven southward from their prime hunting grounds by Comanches and took to raiding the Spaniards partly out of desperation. Not until the mid-1700s would Comanches come close enough to San Antonio to make an impression on colonists there. Before that time, the great confrontation between Spanish and Comanche culture unfolded in and around the bustling trading centers of New Mexico.

Long after Comanches appeared at Taos in 1705, the Spaniards continued to snub them as trading partners. But that only incited raids by Comanches and their allies of the moment, the Utes, who swooped down on settlements in New Mexico and made off with horses and other things they needed to prosper on the Plains. Periodically the raiders struck the Spanish colonists and their Pueblo Indian subjects at Taos and other towns. But the brunt of the attacks fell on Apaches living on the Plains east of the Rio Grande, where Catholic priests had recently established missions. When the Apaches there appealed for help in 1719, Father Juan de la Cruz wrote on their behalf to the viceroy of New Spain, the marqués de Valero, in Mexico City. Father Cruz begged him to protect the missionized Apaches as a way of defending Christianity in a region rife with "heathenism."

Valero was less interested in saving souls than in preserving the settled Apaches as a buffer against enemies—notably the French, who were now at war with Spain in Europe. Rumors had reached Mexico City that the French from their base in Louisiana intended to invade distant New Mexico. Valero authorized military support for the beleaguered Apaches in the hope that they might soon return the favor by helping to thwart the French "and block their evil designs."

This obsession with the French led to two costly Spanish expeditions that did nothing to ease the threat posed by Comanches. In mid-September, the governor of New Mexico, Antonio Valverde, headed out onto the Plains to aid the Apaches with a mixed force of more than 750 Spaniards and Indians, accompanied by a pack-train loaded down with tobacco, chocolate, and other gifts for friendly chiefs as well as a keg of brandy to celebrate saints' days. Valverde found

Richly ornamented, the limestone facade of San Jose Mission in San Antonio helped deter attacks by Apache and Comanche raiders.

that what Spanish colonists called the Apachería was now contested ground. Jicarilla Apaches in northeastern New Mexico, some of whom now lived in adobe homes with irrigated fields, told of losing both their crops and their loved ones to Comanche raiders. In a single attack the year before, Comanches had killed 60 people and carried away 64 women and children. Apaches eager to avenge such raids swelled Valverde's force. They traveled far, reaching the Arkansas River in Colorado and following it eastward toward Kansas, but they saw nothing of Comanches except a few abandoned campsites. With winter fast approaching, Valverde returned to New Mexico in late October, empty handed.

The results should have discouraged the New Mexicans from chasing after shadows, but Valverde brought back a report that prompted an even longer expedition the next year. Near the Arkansas, he had encountered a wounded Apache chief who told of being ambushed while planting corn—not by Comanches but by Pawnees, armed and supported by arrogant Frenchmen, who derided the Spaniards as "women." Piqued, Spanish officials ignored more pressing problems and dispatched a party of more than 100 colonial soldiers and Pueblo auxiliaries from Santa Fe on an epic quest for the Pawnee and their French patrons. The journey ended disastrously along the Platte River in southeastern Nebraska, where Pawnees and allied Indians surprised the soldiers and killed more than 40 of them. Survivors disagreed as to whether Frenchmen had played any part in the attack. But it soon became clear that the real challenge to Spanish authority in New

This 19-foot-long hide painting depicts the massacre of a Spanish expedition in eastern Nebraska in 1720 by a large body of Pawnee and allied warriors. The Spanish force of about 45 Spaniards and 60 Pueblo Indians had marched from Santa Fe to investigate rumors of French activity along the Platte River. Although French soldiers in tricornered hats are shown here firing on the Spaniards, there was no proof of French involvement.

Mexico came not from the distant French but from nearby Comanches.

In the years ahead, Comanches continued to raid the well-stocked Apache villages, or *rancherías,* as the Spaniards called them. Apache bands had long settled in one place during the summer, cultivating small plots of corn and other crops before breaking up into small groups for the rest of the year to roam the Plains in pursuit of buffalo. Now, however, many Apaches in and around New Mexico spent less time hunting and more time in their riverside rancherías and fields. These settlements were easy marks for Comanche raiders, who for their part rarely camped in the same place twice and generally eluded pursuit.

To reach Apache settlements, Comanches traveled up to 400 miles in war parties that often consisted of several hundred men. Each man brought along at least two prime war-horses so that he always had a fresh mount when speed was of the essence. Other horses carried provisions—and sometimes the warriors' wives, who erected base camps near the enemy and even joined in the fighting at times. Comanches were expert at navigating the open grasslands. Once a warrior had traversed a region, he could sketch in the dirt with a pointed stick an accurate map of the terrain, which others could then commit to memory.

Apaches had plenty of horses to attract raiders but fought on foot rather than on horseback. They stood little chance of prevailing when mounted Comanches surrounded a village and closed on the startled occupants in a swirling mass, loosing a steady stream of arrows and dodging

and weaving on their mounts to avoid return fire. Once resistance had crumbled, Comanches destroyed the huts, rounded up the horses, and made off with spoils, including women and children, who would later be traded away or integrated into Comanche society.

Desperate Apaches persisted in seeking Spanish aid, to little effect. Spanish soldiers did manage to rescue some of those who had been taken captive by Comanches. But not even pledges of loyalty from the Jicarillas to the king of Spain could induce the colonial government to assist Apaches by relaxing the official ban on trading firearms to Indians. Unable to withstand the repeated Comanche assaults, Apaches abandoned village after village on the Plains and headed off to the south and west. By 1726 Jicarillas from as far away as Colorado had fled their homes and settled under Spanish protection around Taos and Pecos. Elsewhere, across Kansas, Oklahoma, and the Texas Panhandle, other Apache bands were driven southward from the best buffalo country by Comanches. Many ended up in arid territory near the Rio Grande, where they subsisted partly by raiding other tribes or Spanish settlements. The exodus was largely complete by about 1740, when French traders Pierre and Paul Mallett traveled for several weeks through the heart of the former Apachería without meeting a single Apache.

As proud inheritors of the grasslands, Comanches felt confident enough to dispense with the Utes. Conflict between the two groups evidently flared up in the 1720s. By the 1740s, the Utes had been driven back into their Rocky Mountain homeland. Thereafter they ventured out onto the Plains to stalk buffalo for brief periods only, keeping a sharp eye out for Comanches, whose population was expanding as they flourished as hunters and raiders. "They are a people so numerous and so haughty," Frenchman Athanase de Mézières wrote later in the century, "that when asked their number, they make no difficulty in comparing it to that of the stars."

After overpowering the Jicarilla and other Apache bands, Comanches had a free path to Spanish New Mexico. They still raided the colonists from time to time, but they did not have to fight Spaniards to get what they wanted. Now they could trade if they preferred, for they were no longer excluded from the fairs at Taos and Pecos. Those annual gatherings were raucous affairs. A Spanish priest, Father Pedro Serrano, likened the arrival of hundreds of Comanche traders to the descent of sailors on a port, where they fell prey to profit-minded locals. "Here all prudence forsakes them," he wrote of the colonists, "because the fleet is in." Spaniards took advantage of their Indian guests by levying unauthorized trading fees and by overcharging them. To keep from antagonizing Comanches and losing

The Jicarilla Apaches of eastern New Mexico and Colorado lived in small clusters of tipis like the encampment shown above when they were hunting buffalo and in larger villages along rivers or streams when they were growing crops. The Jicarilla chief (inset) was photographed by Edward Curtis about 1906.

their trade, Spanish authorities set prices and cracked down on shady practices. A tanned buffalo robe—a product of considerable effort on the Indians' part—was valued at a single iron knife, while two robes brought what one Spaniard described as "a very poor bridle," garnished with red rags.

Aside from knives and riding gear, Comanche traders sought horses, tobacco, metal implements, and bright tin religious crosses that warriors favored as charms. The Spaniards, in return, accepted from the Comanches dried buffalo meat as well as hides, which the colonists used themselves or exchanged at the great Chihuahua fair in Mexico for manufactured goods not produced in the province. Spanish officials hoped that such commerce would transform the Comanche into trusted allies who might replace the Apache as a buffer against the French.

Yet there was a sinister side to the trade that did nothing to promote peace. Spaniards in New Mexico had long purchased as slaves Indian captives taken by Apaches, Utes, Comanches, and other combative tribes in the area. Some of these slaves were kept by the colonists as field hands or domestic servants, while others were exported southward to Mexico, where many ended up toiling in mines. Spaniards tried to justify this trade as a way of exposing the slaves to Christianity. In 1714, for example, the governor of New Mexico decreed that all colonists must first baptize the Indian captives they obtained before taking them "to distant places to sell."

Baptism did not keep Indian slaves from being mistreated, however. Boys purchased as ranch hands or house servants were often broken to the task with a whip until they did as they were told. Captive girls and women, for their part, risked abuse both from the Indian raiders who seized them and from the colonists who purchased them, hoping that they would soon produce offspring to enhance the owners' investment. A female slave of prime childbearing age could fetch a price of two good horses, along with some clothing. A woman who had been raped by her captors evidently gained value in the eyes of some purchasers. Father Serrano reported that some young women were violated in the marketplace before they were put up for sale. One Indian trader who abused a captive in this way offered her to the Spaniards with the words: "Now you can take her—now she is good."

For all the cruelty of the trade, both Comanches and Spaniards sometimes took pity on prisoners and treated them well. Captive women and children adopted by warriors as wives and kin sometimes embraced Co-

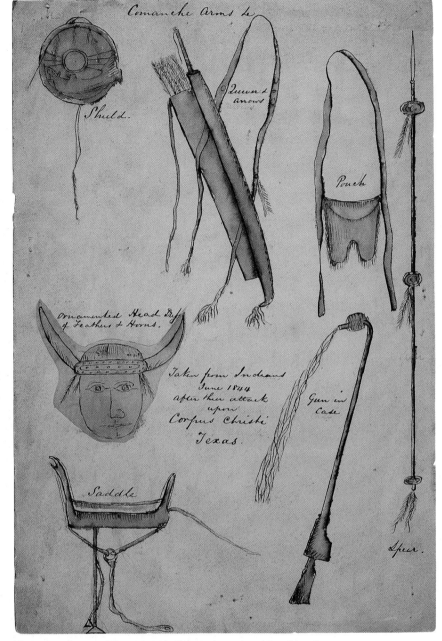

These sketches of a mounted Comanche warrior's equipment were made by a British visitor to Texas in 1844. The warrior's medicine pouch contained protective charms associated with his guardian spirit.

manche ways so heartily that they later declined invitations to return home. Colonists, too, welcomed slaves into their families through marriage or adoption, and they routinely ransomed white prisoners and Indian captives taken from friendly tribes. Whether Spaniards bought captives to free them or to keep them in servitude, however, the deals only encouraged Comanches to collect more prisoners and bring them to market.

Even in relatively tranquil times, Comanche trading was interspersed with raiding. One band might be peaceably engaged in the Taos fair, while another was attacking a frontier settlement to the south. Or the same band might offer captives for sale at Pecos that they had seized from a nearby Spanish or Pueblo outpost. A Spanish priest complained that Comanches always got what they wanted, "by purchase in peace and by theft in war."

In the mid-1740s, the balance tilted toward war. Comanche raiders roamed the Spanish frontier, prompting colonists and Indians to desert exposed farms and villages there. Many fled to Santa Fe, whose population soared. Among the afflicted outposts was Pecos, which lay open to the Plains and the oncoming Comanches. Some 150 Indians and colonists living there died in attacks between 1744 and 1749. Comanches may have been especially hostile to Pecos because a number of their Apache enemies had taken refuge there. As the attacks escalated, officials in New Mexico reluctantly imposed a two-year ban on trading with the Comanche, beginning in 1746. To protect Pecos and Galisteo, another vulnerable outpost nearby, each town was fortified with entrenchments and towers and watched over by troops.

In this latest crisis, the Spaniards again blamed their European rivals, for French muskets were seen in the hands of Comanche warriors. Trading with the French marked a significant departure for the Comanche, who had long resented French dealings with rival tribes such as the Wichita. For some time, Comanche bands along the Arkansas River had been sparring with the Wichita—who were under even greater pressure from the Osage and were retreating southward from their settlements in Kansas. By the 1740s, however, the Wichita had regrouped along the Red River between present-day Oklahoma and Texas, where they built well-fortified villages and trading posts and did a brisk business with the French. Impressed by the resolve of the Wichita and the strength of their positions, Comanche chiefs agreed to a French proposal that they make peace with the tribe and reap the benefits of trade. Soon French guns were filtering through the fortified Wichita villages to Comanches in exchange for hides, horses, and captives, whom Wichitas put to work scraping buffalo hides and raising crops.

BEADED
NECKLACES

STEEL KNIFE

A vibrant trade center known as Pecos Pueblo long occupied this remote site in north-central New Mexico. For centuries Apaches, Comanches, and other Plains dwellers traveled through a pass in the Sangre de Cristo Mountains (background) to trade at Pecos, offering the Spaniards and Pueblo Indians horses, hides, meat, and other things in exchange for useful or alluring items such as those shown here.

TROPICAL BIRD FEATHERS

SPANISH ROSARY

By arming Comanches, the French may have added to Spanish woes in New Mexico. But the real ambition of the French was not to annihilate those colonists but to incorporate them into the French trade network. In 1750 the governor of Louisiana drew up such a proposal for Spanish consideration. He declared in writing that the French were prepared to build warehouses on the Arkansas River and transport goods there by canoe for transit under armed guard to New Mexico. This remarkable document was entrusted to the far-ranging trader Pierre Mallett, who set out for Santa Fe with three other Frenchmen. Approaching Pecos, they crossed paths with more than 100 Comanche warriors, who were out after a band of Pueblo hunters. The Comanches wanted to keep the French trade to themselves and warned Mallett not to barter with Spaniards. To drive home the point, they tore up his document and confiscated most of the traders' goods.

Continuing a tradition dating back to the Spanish colonial era, a huge throng of Indians and white settlers gather in Taos, New Mexico, in 1885 to celebrate the feast of Saint Geronimo, the patron saint of Taos Pueblo, and to attend the town's celebrated trade fair, held on the same day.

When the Frenchmen finally reached Santa Fe and presented their proposal to Governor Tomás Vélez Cachupin, he bristled. The governor, who went by the surname of Vélez, had recently learned of the Comanche-Wichita alliance and suspected that the French planned to use their new ties with the Comanche to destroy New Mexico. He confiscated the traders' remaining goods and shipped the emissaries off to Mexico City for interrogation by the viceroy.

Vélez may have misread French intentions, but he was shrewd enough to recognize that the Comanche might yet be appeased and lured back to the Spanish camp. A young man whom Comanches called the "boy captain," Vélez had already learned much about the tribe by talking to visiting Comanches and by questioning people who had been held captive by them. He knew that some of their chiefs were hostile toward Spaniards, while others were peacefully inclined. During the early summer of 1751, he hosted Comanches at the Taos trade fair. They would be treated well, he assured them, so long as they ceased their attacks on Pecos and Galisteo. If the raids persisted, however, he meant to punish the offenders. The Comanches at Taos pledged cooperation, and Vélez offered them presents and reassurances. The summer passed uneventfully, but some warriors had come to depend on raiding as a source of prestige as well as prizes. In the fall, Comanches again descended on Galisteo, only to be repulsed there by soldiers. The sole losses for the settlement were some cows the Comanches slaughtered.

Although the attack proved ineffectual, Vélez led a force of more than 100 Spaniards and Pueblos in hot pursuit. After a 300-mile chase, they cornered a band of 145 Comanches in a box canyon. The warriors—accompanied by some women and children—refused to surrender. Their opponents then set fire to brush in the canyon and blasted away with their muskets into the night, killing more than 90 Comanches. The survivors were pressed back into a pond, where they risked drowning—a death Comanches dreaded because they believed their spirit would be trapped and prevented from reaching the next world. To avoid that fate, a boy with a wounded foot limped out of the water, carrying a cross he had fashioned from reeds as a token of surrender. Others followed, weeping in terror. In the end, 40 men, six women, and three children gave themselves up. Nearly all of them had been wounded in the deadly assault.

Vélez had his men light fires and wrap the survivors in blankets. Then he kept four of them as hostages, to hasten the return of Spanish captives who were still being held by hostile chiefs, and released the rest to tell their people of the fearful battle. They took with them gifts of tobacco for their leaders—and a demand from the governor that all bands keep the peace. One chief who had staunchly defied the Spaniards took the lead in calling a council of Comanche leaders. They met in December, smoked the governor's tobacco, and decided that it would be better to pursue trade than vengeance. They urged their followers to refrain from raiding and to release Spanish captives. In years to come, Vélez did his best to preserve the peace by personally patrolling the trade fairs and seeing that Comanches were treated fairly. Aware of their admiration for elegant Spanish attire, he appeared at the fairs "adorned with all splendor possible," as he put it. He even appointed an officer to guard the horse herds of visiting Comanches, a favor they appreciated "in the highest degree."

Vélez embodied many of the qualities that Comanches prized in their own chiefs. He could be harsh with opponents. But once he came to terms with them, he kept his word and paid them due respect. Unfortunately this hard-earned understanding between Comanches and Spaniards was neither lasting nor universal. Some of the governors who succeeded Vélez at Santa Fe ignored his example and antagonized the tribe. And the truce arranged in New Mexico was no more binding on the Spanish colonists in Texas than it was on the nearby Comanches. There, both sides still had some painful lessons to learn.

Comanches first appeared at San Antonio in 1743 to inquire about the whereabouts of their enemies, the Lipan Apaches, who had been drifting southward under pressure from Comanche war parties for some time. The visiting Comanches meant no harm to the Spaniards, for both groups were then at odds with the Lipans, who had been raiding colonists in south Texas. But partly through zeal and partly through ignorance, the Spaniards would soon allow themselves to be maneuvered into conflict with Comanches.

One day in 1750, a delegation of Lipan Apaches entered San Antonio and asked to speak with the Brown Robes, as they called the Franciscan friars who ran the missions there. Despite ongoing Apache raids, the Franciscans still hoped to win over the Lipans and convert them to Christianity. Thus they responded with great interest when the Apache delegates invited them to establish a new mission along the San Saba River, 100 miles or so to the north. The Apaches described the area as Lipan country and may well have regarded it as such. But they failed to mention that Comanches were sharply contesting that claim.

For several years, Spaniards debated the merits of this proposal. The priests and their military protectors would be venturing into unknown ter-

Even as late as the 1840s, when George Catlin painted this scene, a Comanche war party was a breathtaking sight. Subsisting on dried meat and water, these legendary horsemen commonly rode hundreds of miles to raid a pueblo or avenge a death. The "tekniwup," or war club (inset), carried by war leaders, symbolized their authority and also served as a weapon.

ritory. On the other hand, establishing a mission and a presidio on the San Saba might bring the troublesome Lipans firmly into the Spanish fold. And there were intriguing rumors of silver deposits in the area. Finally the viceroy in Mexico City endorsed the venture. In April 1757, an expedition of friars and soldiers made the journey from San Antonio to the San Saba, guided by Lipans. Some 3,000 curious Apaches camped near the river as the log structures went up there. The presidio was located three miles from the mission compound to prevent undesirable contacts between soldiers and Indian converts.

The Lipans evidently hoped that the Spanish presence would render the area secure against Comanches. But the nearby Apaches declined to enter the mission when it was completed. After accepting presents from the priests, they left to hunt buffalo to the north, where their enemies abounded. The Apaches returned later that fall with plenty of meat but stayed only a few days. Their hurried departure suggested that they had clashed with their northern foes and feared reprisals.

A few months later, at dawn on March 16, 1758, a formidable force of mounted warriors descended on the San Saba mission—some 2,000 men in all, mainly Comanches and allied Wichitas, along with some Hasinais and Tonkawas. Mutual trading ties with the French may have encouraged this unlikely coalition, made up of groups that had often been at odds in the past but now seemed to be united in their hostility to Apaches and to those who aided them. Many of the warriors carried French muskets. Their faces were painted for battle with streaks of red and black and they wore a variety of headdresses, some topped with plumes, others with deer antlers or with the bison horns favored by Comanches. Most were dressed in traditional fashion, but one Comanche chief wore a red jacket that looked to the anxious Spaniards like a French army uniform.

With face and legs painted, a Comanche warrior holds a rifle in a fringed case. Among the Comanche, both women and men painted their faces before confronting strangers and on other special occasions.

As warriors surrounded the mission compound, some of them gestured to the priests and their guards in sign language that the Spaniards could understand. They asked to be admitted, indicating that they sought only the Apaches who had slain some of their people. Once inside the compound, they accepted presents from the priests—or simply took what they wanted. Hoping to avert bloodshed, the father superior of the mission, Father Alonso Giraldo de Terreros, stood by without protest as warriors seized horses from the stables. Terreros even wrote a note to the commander of the presidio, Colonel Diego Ortiz Parrilla, urging him to oblige the Indians in similar fashion. As warriors rode to the presidio with this message, however, they were met by a party of soldiers hurrying to defend the mission. Fighting erupted, and the Spaniards were overwhelmed. When the victors rode back to the mission waving the soldiers' scalps, the warriors milling about there attacked, killing Father Terreros and seven others in the compound and wounding many more. The Indians later made off with booty from the mission but left the presidio untouched.

The Spaniards had invited this disaster by blundering into the middle of a bitter intertribal dispute. But they chose to blame the Comanche and their allies—backed, presumably, by the nefarious French—and embarked on a punitive campaign. In August 1759, a large force marched northward out of San Antonio under the command of Colonel Parrilla, a seasoned officer from Spain who had fought in Morocco against the Moors. The column grew to include some 600 men, including 134 Lipans. In early October, Parrilla's force surprised an encampment of Tonkawas on the Brazos River and attacked, killing 55 people and capturing 149. Afterward the Spaniards found mules bearing the San Saba brand in the camp and fragments of a priest's robe, suggesting that warriors there had joined in attacking the mission.

Some of the captives led Parrilla northward to the vicinity of the Red River, where his men came up against a stoutly fortified Wichita village on the river's south bank. The occupants of this stronghold had dug a moat around it and piled up the earth against a stockade. Within the walls stood the oval grass houses of the Wichita and the tipis of their Comanche allies. Waiting to defend the village were no fewer than 2,000 warriors, well armed with muskets and other weapons.

Parrilla opened fire with his two cannon. Each shot thudded without effect against the thick earthen embankment, eliciting taunts from the defenders, who kept up a steady fire from atop the earthworks and from horseback in front of the village. Each rider with a musket was supported

This painting details the 1758 assault at San Saba, Texas, where Franciscans had built a mission for Lipan Apaches. Angered by the Apache-Spanish alliance, 2,000 Comanche and allied warriors—led by a chief shown here wearing a red coat and carrying a white flag—pillaged the mission, killing eight people, including the father superior, Alonso Giraldo de Terreros (left) and another missionary, Father Santiesteban (right).

by two attendants on foot, who reloaded for him so that he could keep firing. Small detachments also rode out to counterattack. These were tactics the Spaniards had "never before experienced among the Indians," reported Antonio Bonilla, an officer who studied reports of the battle. Whether the defenders had learned from the French or had evolved these techniques on their own, it was a triumph of adaptation. As Bonilla put it, their way of fighting "so astounded Parrilla's troops that this officer's ardor, good example, and persuasions were of no avail." Indeed, some of his Spanish troops hesitated, and many of his Indian auxiliaries fled.

Darkness brought an end to the contest after four hours. Inside the stockade that night, bonfires were kindled, and warriors celebrated their success. Parrilla, who had twice been grazed by bullets and had his horse shot from under him, pulled back during the night and decided the next day to end the campaign. To lighten his retreat, he abandoned the two cannon to the foe. He estimated nearly 50 enemy dead against 19 of his own. Despite the strength of the fortifications, the battle was seen as a humiliating defeat for the Spaniards. Ironically, the Indian village they had failed to take became known as the Spanish Fort.

Summoned to Mexico City, Parrilla faced a court-martial. In his testimony, he attributed the setback to French interference. Only French officers could have organized such defenses, he and others claimed. Some Spaniards told of seeing the French flag flying over the village. In convicting Parrilla, however, the court found no evidence of French involvement beyond the presence of a few traders.

In fact the rivalry between France and Spain was much diminished. The two groups now recognized a common foe in the British and their expanding colonies in North America. In 1763 France conceded defeat to Great Britain in the French and Indian War and ceased to be a major power in the New World. Although some French traders remained in the Southwest, the Spaniards had to give up their old habit of blaming Indian opposition on French schemes. The Comanche were now recognized in San Antonio as powerful foes in their own right.

Comanches, in turn, had come to regard the Spaniards in Texas as an enemy people—and a vulnerable one at that. Raiders began to target Spanish outposts on either side of the Rio Grande. They struck swiftly and from long distances, focusing on isolated settlements and ranches and avoiding forts. Their main encampments remained in the heart of buffalo country, up around the Texas Panhandle. Spanish military contingents, recalling the fate of Colonel Parrilla, rarely ventured north to challenge the Comanches there. In fact the frontier was so rife with raiders that even heavily armed companies of cavalry had to dip south into Mexico to get from San Antonio to Santa Fe.

In New Mexico, meanwhile, the peace fostered by Governor Vélez had been shattered. In 1760 a large force of Comanche raiders—incited by Taos Indians who danced at the local trade fair waving Comanche scalps—raided ranches in the area, killing the men and capturing 56 women and children. A year later, hundreds of Comanches approached Taos with seven of the prisoners in the hope of using them to arrange a truce. Chiefs who appealed to Governor Manuel del Portillo, however, were threatened with death if they did not release the captives at once. They freed six women but declined to turn over the seventh prisoner, a boy, insisting that he did not wish to leave those who had taken him in. At that, Portillo encircled the Comanche camp with a combined force of Spaniards, Pueblos, and Utes and had the boy seized. Comanches lashed out at the surrounding force and were cut down by musketry and cannon

Eddy Burgess (right) sits astride his mount at the 1993 Comanche Nation Fair in the proud tradition of earlier generations of Comanche horsemen (above, left). His breastplate, a token of distinction, is similar to the l9th-century example at top right.

fire. The battle claimed the lives of all 200 men in the camp and left their women and children in Spanish hands.

Portillo's provocative deed incited Comanche bands to prepare for a war of revenge against the colonists. Officials in Mexico City averted disaster by removing Portillo and replacing him with Tomas Vélez, who embarked on his second term as governor by inviting Comanche leaders to Santa Fe, smoking peace pipes with them, and negotiating an exchange of prisoners. Once more, Comanches had a governor they could deal with. But the old animosities revived after Vélez stepped down in 1767. His successor was far less diplomatic and tried to force Comanches into line—which only strengthened the hand of chiefs who welcomed hostilities.

Two of the boldest Comanche war leaders during this period came from one family. The father was known to his Spanish foes as Cuerno Verde, or Green Horn, for that distinctive feature of his headdress. One Spanish observer noted that he had other regal accouterments, including guards to protect him and attendants to shield him from the sun by holding over his head a "shade of buffalo skins."

In 1768, during a raid on the settlement of Ojo Caliente, north of Santa Fe, Green Horn was shot down. His son took up the slain father's headdress and became the second Green Horn, embarking on a decade-long

Adobe churches like the one above, shown from both an interior and an exterior view, dominated the plazas of the small Spanish settlements throughout New Mexico. This one, built in 1811, is located in the village of Ojo Caliente, about 25 miles southwest of Taos. Ojo Caliente was the target of numerous Comanche raids.

vendetta against the colonists. He was described as "a cruel scourge of the kingdom, who had exterminated many pueblos, killing hundreds."

The author of that description was Governor Juan Bautista de Anza, an avid soldier and administrator whose father and grandfather had died fighting Apaches. He arrived in Santa Fe in 1778 to take charge of the embattled colony. His orders were to reach an accommodation with the Comanche, which meant first convincing them of Spanish might and then negotiating with them. Green Horn's raiders had been busy that summer, killing or capturing 127 New Mexicans in a sweep through outlying settlements. To win the peace, Anza believed that he had to deal a sharp blow to Green Horn and his followers. He planned to do as Comanches did and strike at his opponents in the heart of their country. Many of those raiding New Mexico started out from near the Arkansas River in Colorado, and it was there that Anza headed.

He set out in August 1779 with nearly 600 Spaniards and Pueblos. He was soon joined by 200 Utes and Jicarilla Apaches, who knew some of the enemy camping places and wanted to settle old scores. To avoid detection, Anza shunned the traditional route to the Arkansas River across the Plains and instead moved due north through the Ute-controlled San Luis Valley. On August 31, along Fountain Creek, near present-day Pueblo, Colorado, his scouts spied a large group of Comanches setting up camp. As Anza's men moved up to attack, the Comanches fled together on horseback. In the chase that followed, the Comanches bringing up the rear bravely turned on their pursuers and held them off long enough for many of their people to get away. Eighteen Comanches died in the fighting, and 34 women and children were captured. Most of them declined to tell Anza's interrogators anything of importance, but the governor at last gleaned some precious intelligence. The Comanches he had attacked were awaiting the return of warriors who had recently joined Green Horn on a raid against Taos.

As the governor was pondering this information that night and his forces were dividing up spoils from the attack, Green Horn and his men were retreating empty handed from Taos, whose defenders had anticipated his approach. The chief was smarting from that rebuff. And he was further aggrieved when a messenger reached him on the trail with word of the attack at Fountain Creek. He could only hope that he would soon have a chance to challenge the nettlesome Spaniards.

Up ahead, near a mountain that would be named for the chief, Anza was ready to oblige him. Anza had followed the chief's trail south, "to see if fortune would grant me an encounter with him." On September 2, his scouts spotted Green Horn's party approaching, and Anza deployed his men in ambush. Some of the Comanches fell into the trap that evening and lost their lives, but Green Horn and the bulk of his men managed to get away.

The chief regrouped and returned the next morning to fight. Wearing his prominent headdress, he rode out in front of his guards, leading 50 men against an overwhelming force of nearly 600. Anza's forces soon cut off Green Horn and his retinue from the others and trapped them in a ravine, where the Comanches dismounted and fought furiously from behind their downed horses. The chief, wrote Anza, kept his dignity to the end, "disdaining even to load his own musket, which was done for him three times by another." All the Comanches in the ravine perished, in a show of defiance

Anza deemed "as brave as it was glorious." Among the dead were the chief, his firstborn son, 14 other warriors, and a medicine man who had declared Green Horn invulnerable. Anza claimed his headdress as a trophy.

Even after this stinging defeat, Comanches were in no hurry to make peace. In 1783 Anza renewed his deadly strikes into the Comanchería. Those attacks came in the wake of an epidemic of smallpox that spread to Comanches through the Wichita trading villages. Weakened by disease and conflict and eager to resume their trade with New Mexico, which Anza had suspended, Comanche delegates traveled to Taos under a white flag during the summer of 1785. Anza declined to deal with them, realizing that an agreement reached with one group might well be ignored by others. He announced that he was ready to negotiate a peace treaty and resume trade, but only if all Comanche bands in the area ratified the accord.

Anza's prodding helped further a process of political consolidation that was already under way among the Comanche. For some time, neighboring Comanche bands had been coalescing into divisions, whose chiefs exercised wide influence. In recent years, for example, a war leader named Toro Blanco, or White Bull, had gained great authority among the northernmost Comanche division, the Yamparika, who dominated the area near the Arkansas River. White Bull was intent on continuing hostilities with the colonists. But in a rare confrontation within the tribe, Comanches who favored peace defied and killed him. His death removed the last great obstacle to the negotiations sought by a rival Yamparika chief, known to the Spaniards as Ecueracapa, or Leather Jacket, for the protective coat of Spanish design some Comanches had adopted. Like White Bull, Leather Jacket was an avid warrior, but he also possessed great diplomatic skills that enabled him to bring Comanches together in pursuit of peace when he saw nothing more to be gained by fighting.

In the autumn of 1785, he summoned representatives from more than 600 Comanche camps—including bands of the Yamparika and their southern neighbors, the Kotsoteka—to a council on the Arkansas River. The delegates confirmed the right of Leather Jacket to serve as their leader in talks with Anza. In February 1786, the two men concluded a landmark peace treaty at Pecos. In return for halting their raids against New Mexico and allying themselves with the Spaniards, Comanches received full trading privileges and the right to live on New Mexican territory. The 200 Comanche leaders present were further gratified when Anza announced he was raising the value of a buffalo hide to two knives. They responded by ceremonially digging and refilling a hole to signify the burial of old animosities. One

of them freed a captive from Santa Fe named Ale-
jandro Martin, who had been held for 11 years.

Anza did much to promote Leather Jacket as
supreme chief. He bestowed on him a saber and
other symbols of office, granted him the right to
travel to Santa Fe at any time to present grievances,
and adhered to an Indian custom for reinforcing
pacts by taking the chief's 20-year-old son into his
home, where the young man learned Spanish.

The treaty heralded more than a generation of
peace in New Mexico, during which further benefits
accrued to Comanches. They were now allowed to
trade for muskets. And officials freely granted guns
and ammunition, horses, and even gifts of cash to
the principal chiefs in exchange for their help in dealing with Apaches to the south, whose raids on the
colonists persisted. Comanches no longer had to
travel to the trade fairs to barter for Spanish goods.
They welcomed to their encampments Spanish and

Comanches.

Comanches du Texas Occidental, vetement lorsqu'ils sont
en paix.

Pueblo traders, known as comancheros, who brought far-flung Comanches
useful items such as wool blankets and metal bridle bits—and introduced
them to the Spanish language and culture. In a sharp break with tradition,
one Comanche chief went so far as to settle down with some of his followers along the Arkansas River in 1787 in houses built there by New Mexican
craftsmen. Anza sent them sheep, oxen, and seeds to plant. But a short
time later, one of the chief's favorite wives died, and the Comanches adhered to custom by abandoning the site of her death, never to return.

During this period, Comanches became embroiled in a bitter feud with
Pawnees, north of the Arkansas. In 1793 Leather Jacket himself led an attack on those enemies and fell gravely wounded. The governor in Santa Fe
sent the town's only medical man, a pharmacist, out onto the Plains to attend to the chief, but no medicine could save him. Afterward Comanche
leaders invited the governor to attend an encampment of 4,500 tribesmen
on the Canadian River, where Leather Jacket's successor as supreme chief
was chosen, ensuring continued stability on the New Mexican frontier.

Peace was harder to come by on the Texas frontier, where colonists
remained prey to raids by far-ranging Comanches, many of whom
claimed horses and other prizes from the Texans and sold them to obliging New Mexicans. Authorities in San Antonio tried to placate Comanche

Yamparicas

Comanches.

Comanches du Texas Occidental: vitement lorsqu'ils vont à la guerre.

Comanches display traditional weapons and apparel along with firearms and other European wares in these watercolors by Mexican artist Lino Sánchez y Tapia, based on sketches by members of a Mexican expedition who met with the Yamparika and other Comanche groups in the 1820s.

chiefs by offering them gifts of tobacco and clothing and by joining them in campaigns against still-defiant Lipans along the Rio Grande. Eventually some of the Comanches living in Texas began to look kindly on visitors from San Antonio—as Captain Francisco Amangual discovered on his trip across the Comanchería in 1808. Forty years earlier, Spaniards would scarcely have considered such a venture. Even as the two sides learned to cope with each other, however, newcomers were impinging on the region and altering the balance of power. Before long, the terms Comanches and Spaniards had arrived at so painfully would cease to apply.

Among the tribal groups who intruded on the southern Plains about this time were the Kiowa, who reached the Arkansas River from the north in the late 1700s. Although they clashed with the Comanche at first, their differences were soon resolved. According to Kiowa lore, peace was initiated when separate parties of Kiowas and Comanches stopped at the house of a New Mexican trader, who was on good terms with both peoples and urged them to set aside their differences. A Comanche chief, Afraid of Water, invited his Kiowa counterpart, Wolf Lying Down, to spend the sum-

Clermont, the Osage chief who led a devastating assault on Kiowas in 1833, holds a huge gunstock war club as an emblem of his authority in this 1834 painting by Catlin. His leggings are adorned with hair from enemy scalps.

mer in his camp among the Yamparika. Wolf Lying Down, the Kiowa's second-ranking chief, agreed to go but told his warriors to return to the trader's house in early autumn. If he was not there, they should avenge him. The Kiowa chief was regally entertained at the Comanche encampment that summer. In the fall, he met his men in New Mexico as promised, but he did not tarry. He returned to the Comanches to live with the daughter of Afraid of Water, thus healing the wounds between the two rivals through the age-old remedy of marriage.

However the alliance came about, it proved lasting. Kiowas and kindred Kiowa Apaches lived amicably near the Yamparika and Kotsoteka Comanche, between the Arkansas and Red Rivers. Sometimes they joined those northern Comanches on expeditions. At other times, they went off on their own, ranging far to the south and west to hunt, trade, or raid. Kiowa lore celebrates one band that rode down through Mexico to Central America, returning with tales of fabulous creatures living in the trees—monkeys and birds of exotic plumage.

Both the Kiowa and their Comanche allies would soon be affected by another group of intruders—the Anglo-Americans—and by tribes these whites displaced. In 1803, through the Louisiana Purchase, France ceded to the United States a vast and vaguely defined area west of the Mississippi that the French retained little control over. The treaty did not pertain to Spanish-held Texas and New Mexico—destined to become territories of an independent Mexico—but it formed the basis for American claims to much of the surrounding area, including Louisiana, Arkansas, Missouri, Kansas, and Oklahoma (known originally as the Indian Territory). In years to come, American settlers surged westward across the Mississippi, uprooting woodlands Indians, who in turn pressed against tribes at the edge of the Plains.

Among those affected were the Osage, whose domain extended from southwestern Missouri into neighboring parts of Arkansas, Oklahoma, and Kansas. Never ones to shrink from a challenge, the Osage responded by defying encroaching whites as well as Indians. Missouri's acting governor, Frederick Bates, described Osage raids on settlers there in 1808: "There was no personal violence offered, but the most wanton waste committed on property of every description. Furniture was split to pieces with their tomahawks; feather beds ript open and destroyed, and every thing which could not be carried away rendered useless."

Bates was indignant and called for reprisals. But Osage warriors had in fact shown restraint in not claiming lives or captives, as they often did when raiding tribal foes. Apparently they wanted to punish the intruding Americans without provoking an all-out war. They could ill afford such conflict, for they had tribal enemies all around and needed firearms and other trade goods. They would have been content if these whites, like their French predecessors, had come simply to trade. But Americans insisted on controlling the land, and the Osage reluctantly agreed to cede large chunks of their territory to the United States in a series of treaties.

The first agreement, in 1808, involved some 200 square miles in southern Missouri and northern Arkansas. Among those who poured into the ceded area were whites and displaced Indians from the East, many of them Cherokees. Fierce blows were exchanged between those Cherokees and nearby Osages. On one occasion, in 1817, the Osage chief Clermont and his men returned from a buffalo hunt on the Plains to their village in eastern Oklahoma to find nearly 40 people there massacred by Cherokees and as many as 100 hauled away as captives. With such powerful new enemies to contend with, the Osage were in no position to defy the United States government. In 1818 and again in 1825, they yielded to fresh territorial demands from federal negotiators.

Osages displaced by the treaties were allotted a reservation in southern Kansas. Members of the tribe who moved there from Missouri or Arkansas found themselves closer to buffalo country. But that benefit was offset by the proximity of hostile Kiowas and Comanches. Indeed the western end of the Osage reservation lay on the open Plains south of the Arkansas River—country that Kiowas and Comanches regarded as their own. In earlier years, Osages who journeyed west to hunt buffalo had clashed periodically with Comanche and Kiowa war parties. Now the con-

After attacking the Kiowa camp, Clermont's raiders placed the severed heads of their victims in brass buckets, including the one shown below.

flict intensified, with war parties confronting each other on the Plains or descending on the vulnerable encampments of their enemies.

One of the hardest blows was struck by Osage raiders in 1833. A party of 300 men led by Clermont came upon a Kiowa village on Rainy Mountain Creek in western Oklahoma. Most of the Kiowa warriors were away fighting Utes, and Clermont struck the exposed camp, just as others had done to the Osage. His warriors killed a number of old men, women, and children, then beheaded several of them and placed the heads in brass buckets to shock Kiowas when they returned. Along with horses and other loot, they took captive a young girl and her brother and carried off the sacred image that was vital to the Kiowa Sun Dance—the taime. Enraged, Kiowas and allied Comanches prowled the Plains in search of the foe. Their vigilance kept the Osage from reaching their favorite hunting grounds along the Canadian and Cimarron Rivers that autumn. Kiowa warriors were so intent on regaining their taime that they took the rare

Reining in his rearing horse, a Comanche war chief signals his peaceful intentions to U.S. troops by waving a piece of white buffalo skin on the point of his lance in this 1834 painting by George Catlin. The artist called the scene "one of the most thrilling and beautiful" he had ever witnessed.

step of invading Osage country in search of Clermont's band. They came to blows with an Osage war party, but a thunderstorm erupted mid-battle and scattered both sides. By the following summer, the U.S. Army was so concerned by the escalating conflict that it dispatched a column of 500 cavalrymen under Colonel Henry Irving Dodge on a peacekeeping mission. Their goal was to establish friendly relations with the Comanche and Kiowa and reconcile them to the Osage and other tribes that the United States had displaced by treaty to make room for American settlers.

Heading west from Fort Gibson near present-day Muskogee, the troops came upon a large Comanche encampment on the open Plains north of the Red River. Dodge and his men, accompanied by artist George Catlin, were impressed by the herd of 3,000 horses surrounding the village and surprised to see the U.S. flag fluttering above the lodges. But most of all, they were struck by the poise of the warriors who came out to meet them. At first, noted Catlin, the troopers and warriors confronted each other warily at a distance of 20 or 30 yards like "inveterate foes." But the Comanches were unarmed, and their leaders offered every sign of friendship. "The head chief galloped up to Colonel Dodge," Catlin noted, "and having shaken him by the hand, he passed on to the other officers in turn."

With no reason as yet to regard the bluecoats as hostile, the Comanche did all they could to oblige Colonel Dodge. In peace parleys held that year and the following summer, Comanches, Kiowas, and allied Wichitas pledged peace to the Americans and came to terms with the Osage. The Kiowa got back their captives and their sacred taime, and the Osage won the right to trade with their former enemies. For years to come, Comanches met amicably with Osage traders on the Plains and offered them horses and mules in exchange for firearms and other goods of American origin.

Colonel Dodge and his superiors had reason to be pleased with this diplomatic breakthrough. But it was as much a Comanche coup as an American one. From the beginning, the alert Comanches had invited peace by flying the American flag and welcoming the troops. Schooled by long experience with white men and their ways, they had calculated that they would gain more by befriending the bluecoats than by fighting them. It was this talent for conciliation, as much as their genius for combat, that enabled Comanches to adhere to their heartland at a time of great tribal upheaval. Yet their future was far from secure. In the northern part of their domain, they remained in firm control. But they faced an unprecedented challenge down south, where Anglo-Texans were on the rise and threatened to supplant the Comanche one day as lords of the Plains. ◆

MEMORIES OF A WARRIOR

A band of Kiowas spend a hot summer day relaxing outside their tipis under sunshades made of blankets. The Wichita Mountains are in the background. The painted tipis belong to men of status who decorated them with designs symbolic of the spiritual power they had received through their visions.

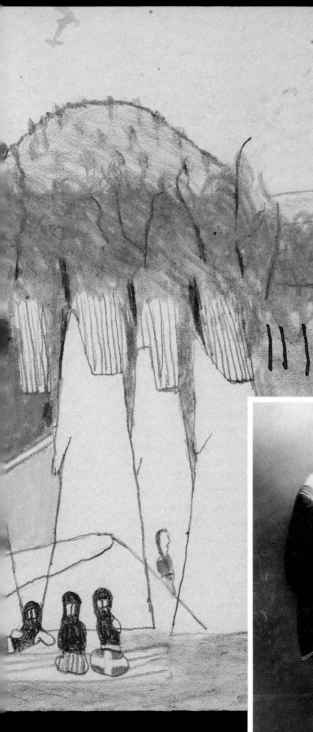

S ince Native American hunters first drew images on buffalo hides centuries ago, art has served as both a tribal record and a way to validate individual achievements. The Kiowa warrior Gu-hau-de, or Wolf Robe, born in 1855, continued the tradition of his ancestors by creating in a white man's drawing book a rich pictorial legacy of life on the southern Plains.

Unlike some other Plains tribes who had strong ties to white traders, the Kiowa of what is today western Oklahoma clung fiercely to their customary lifeways throughout most of the 19th century. A member of the last generation to follow the buffalo, Gu-hau-de gained honors as a hunter and fighter. His career as a warrior ended in 1874 when he was arrested with a group of Kiowas charged with participating in an attack that claimed three lives. While he was in custody, his name was mistakenly recorded as Wohaw, the title by which he was known for the remainder of his life.

Imprisoned for three years at Fort Marion, Florida, Wohaw passed the time drawing detailed scenes from his youth. By the end of his incarceration, he had produced an impressive firsthand account of Kiowa life. Wohaw returned to the West in 1878 to find his kinspeople confined on a reservation and the buffalo virtually exterminated. His brilliantly colored line drawings remain as an eloquent testimony to the vibrancy of his tribe's traditional life.

Wohaw appears in 1890, at age 35, in a combination of Indian and European dress. After his release from prison, he served in the Indian police force at Fort Sill and later in the U.S. Cavalry. In 1900 he received 160 acres on the Kiowa Reservation in present-day Oklahoma but refused to become a farmer. Instead he leased the land to whites. He died in 1924.

IN PURSUIT OF PREY

Men stand on either side of a freshly killed buffalo while two women, tools in hand, prepare to butcher the animal (above). Afterward, the hunter and his wives pack the meat in the animal's hide and carry it home for drying (right). Many Kiowa men had two wives to help fulfill the numerous domestic tasks that were assigned to women.

Their gear stowed in the bushes, three warriors cook the meat of a buffalo over a fire. The horns and part of the carcass of the animal can be seen over the ridge at top left beyond a trail of half-moon-shaped hoofprints left by a horse. The identity of the couple in the distance is unclear.

1882.18.37

DESTINED FOR BATTLE

A war society leader dressed in full regalia raises his pipe. Wohaw is holding the reins of his mount and his bow. The horse's tail is bound with cloth, a traditional preparation for war. While at Fort Marion, Wohaw acquired a knowledge of English. He has printed his name on this drawing to identify himself.

Spotted with blue war paint to protect him in battle, a horse awaits his rider. The string of bells is a decoration. A warrior with a T-shaped design painted across the lower half of his face stands nearby. Wohaw has faithfully recorded details of the warrior's apparel, including his breastplate.

A Kiowa war party heads off on a raid. The war bonnets, lances, and guidons indicate that all are men of status. Extra horses were always brought along so that the warriors could maintain fresh mounts. The leading rider wears a red cape, similar to those worn today by members of the Black Legs, a Kiowa military society, to commemorate a 19th-century warrior who killed a Mexican militiaman and took his cape as a trophy.

FORGING AN ALLIANCE

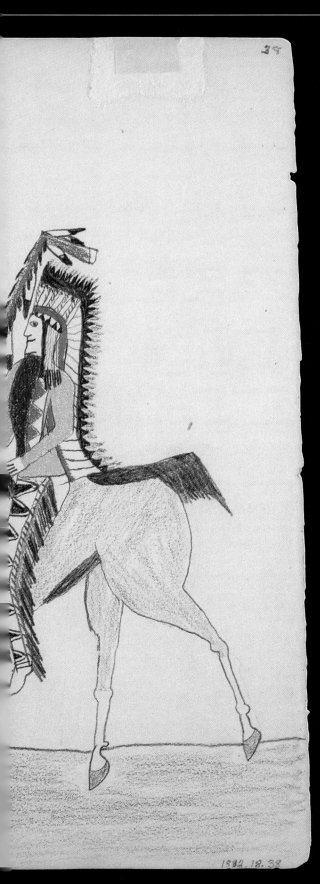

This drawing may represent a parley that took place in March 1873 when the Pawnee leader Lone Chief (wearing a buffalo-horn headdress and carrying a sword) came to seek peace with the Kiowa chief Kicking Bird (wearing a war bonnet and holding a tomahawk). Both men have an arm outstretched in greeting. Thomas Battey, a Quaker who lived among the Kiowa, recalled that the tribes sealed the alliance with gifts: The Pawnee offered shawls and blankets; the Kiowa, sticks, each of which represented a pony to be supplied when the visitors departed.

VIEWS OF THE SUN DANCE

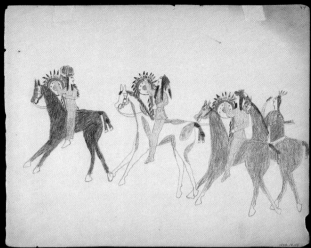

The Sun Dance was as much a social occasion as it was a religious celebration. In these three drawings, Wohaw depicts some of the courting, hunting, and parading that occurred when the entire Kiowa tribe gathered together. In the drawing at far left, two unchaperoned girls flirt with a warrior, while another girl meets a possible suitor beside a tree. The hunting scene possibly shows the slain yearling "medicine" buffalo whose hide will be used in the ceremony, or simply an ordinary bison slain to provide meat for feasting. In the drawing above, members of a ceremonial shield society display their shields with a common motif.

Gathered under an arbor, a Kiowa family welcomes an elaborately dressed visitor during the Sun Dance, a 10-day period of spiritual and tribal renewal held about the time of the summer solstice.

Painted yellow and with sacred sage tied to his wrists, the keeper of the taime stands outside the Sun Dance lodge and asks Thunderbird to transfer power to the taime placed on the stake behind him. Unwrapped from its deerskin pouch only during the Sun Dance, the taime is a human figure carved in stone. A symbolic buffalo made from sticks and the yearling medicine hide have been placed atop the lodge.

Members of a Kiowa warrior society gather during the Sun Dance. The ceremony was the time when new members were invited to join their ranks. The Kiowa had six military societies, each of which had its own rattles, lances, and other special accouterments. After Wohaw's release from prison, he joined the Ohoma Society and frequently danced with an army saber.

1852.18.36

The beadwork of a
fringed pouch used
to hold a peyote
button depicts the
button as it appears
during worship.

THE PEYOTE ROAD

In the 1890s, peyote leaders from the Kiowa-Comanche-Apache reservation in Oklahoma display the water drum, gourd rattle, feathered fan, and wooden staff that are the primary instruments of the peyote ritual. Only the rounded pincushion-like tops of the turnip-sized peyote cactus (inset) grow above the soil. The tops are cut off and dried into buttons that are later consumed ritually.

During the years following the Civil War, the demise of the buffalo and relentless white expansion onto Indian lands threatened the peoples of the southern Plains with the extinction of their way of life. Facing cultural catastrophe, some Plains groups found relief in a religious ceremony involving peyote, a small, spineless cactus that produces a hallucinogenic effect when ingested. Peyote grows wild in the chalky soils of the Rio Grande Valley and areas to the south. Since Aztec times, the native peoples of Mexico have used it as a means to cure, prophesy, and pray. Apache bands probably brought the cactus northward to the Plains, where its ritual use, known as the Peyote Road, spread rapidly.

Combining traditional sacred practices with certain aspects of Christianity, the standard Plains peyote meeting took place at night inside a special tipi around a ceremonial fire and a crescent-shaped altar of raised earth. A leader known as a road chief, or roadman, officiated, assisted by a fire tender and drummer. After various smoking and purifying rituals, the dozen or so worshipers passed around peyote emblems and instruments, reverently ate peyote tops, or buttons, and sang peyote songs to gain spirit power. The ceremony ended at dawn when the celebrants shared a ritual breakfast.

Charismatic roadmen such as the great Comanche chief Quanah Parker spread the religion beyond the southern Plains to tribes of many regions. In 1918 the ritual was legally incorporated as the Native American Church, an intertribal institution that still plays a major role in the fight for Indian religious freedom. Peyotists, who today number more than 250,000, believe that God created the plant for the exclusive use of the Indians in order to show them the correct way of life.

INSTRUMENTS OF DEVOTION

Five worshipers in a peyote tipi sit west of a fireplace framed by a crescent-shaped altar fashioned of mounded earth. The altar symbolizes the mountain range where, according to oral tradition, Peyote Woman first discovered the cactus. The fire, used for burning cedar incense and other rites, is kept constantly alight during the course of the ceremony, even on the hottest summer nights.

Geometric beadwork adorns the handle of a Kiowa fan. The feathers represent birds that carry the worshiper's prayers to the Creator.

A water drum like the one at left, made by stretching hide over a kettle, is used to accompany peyote prayer songs.

Symbols of peyote buttons decorate an Osage turban made of otter fur. Until recently such headgear was standard regalia for Osage Peyotists.

Peyote rattles, like this Comanche example, are made from a variety of gourd cultivated on the southern Plains.

This staff, shown disassembled with sacred objects on the top half, represents the sacred authority of the peyote leader, or roadman.

THE SACRED MEETING PLACE

As shown here, the peyote tipi is made to be taken down and reassembled as required. Particular care is devoted to ensure that the cover fits tightly over the poles. The door of the ceremonial lodge always faces east.

A roadman, drummer, and fire tender enter a peyote tipi to begin a peyote ceremony in this 1891 drawing by Silverhorn, a Kiowa artist. Silverhorn's drawings of that year are believed to be the earliest Indian depictions of Peyotism; they show many aspects of the meetings that are still practiced today.

A roadman sits in his customary spot behind the crescent-shaped altar in this drawing by Silverhorn. The roadman begins the ceremony by placing a large peyote button, called the Peyote Chief, or Grandfather Peyote, upon the altar and singing the opening prayer songs.

This hide painting, also by Silverhorn, shows male and female worshipers seated around the altar and ritual fire on blankets placed over a bed of fragrant purple sage. The man with his arm outstretched at left is preparing to eat the first of four peyote buttons.

About midnight, the fire tender leaves the tipi and returns with a bucket of water for refreshment and for use in the ceremony. He carries an eagle feather as an amulet of protection. Prayers are said over the water for the success of the meeting, and the singing and praying resume. This drawing as well as the others shown here are Silverhorn's.

A water woman in her finest attire brings more water to the tipi at first light of dawn. At the roadman's signal, she will bring in the water and say her own prayers. At this point in the meeting, curing rites are sometimes practiced.

A woman stands outside the tipi with the ritual breakfast arranged in special order. It consists of corn, meat, fruit, and a sweet. The 1892 photograph at right shows a Kiowa breakfast laid out before the altar.

Two worshipers leave the peyote tent following the closing songs. Participants must circle clockwise around the altar before exiting.

AN ENDURING FAITH

Morning sunlight streams through a tipi door after a peyote meeting at the 1993 Comanche Nation Fair. Ashes from the ceremonial fire have been ritually arranged to follow the shape of the earthen altar.

Comanche Peyotists carefully disassemble the prayer tipi following the conclusion of the ceremony. A celebratory feast, which is hosted by the sponsor of the meeting, often takes place after the peyote service.

An enamelware bucket used in modern peyote ceremonies is decorated with paintings of a large peyote button, a rattle, staff, drum, and two fans.

127

A peyote button, an altar, and the feathers of the peyote fan are among the symbols incised into a Peyotist's neckerchief slide.

A painting made in 1925 by the Kiowa artist Stephen Mopope pays tribute to the early peyote roadman of the southern Plains. Mopope, who acknowledged Silverhorn as his first teacher, achieved international acclaim as an artist.

3

THE STRUGGLE FOR TEXAS

Comanche leader Quanah Parker sits for a portrait in his home about 1890, clad in traditional finery and flanked by images of his white mother, Cynthia Ann Parker, and her Christian faith. In his early years, Quanah followed in the path of his Comanche father and led war parties against whites. Later he accepted reservation life and worked peacefully on behalf of Comanches.

In the spring of 1836, two violent events unfolded that had profound consequences for Indians of the southern Plains. In April a small army of Texans, most of them recent immigrants of Anglo-American stock, won independence from Mexico with a crushing victory at San Jacinto, near present-day Houston. After storming the enemy camp, Texans went on a rampage, slaughtering wounded Mexicans who were unable to resist as well as men who fought back. The victors saw the massacre as retribution for harsh deeds committed recently by their Mexican foes, including a notorious incident at San Antonio—the virtual annihilation of the Texans defending the Alamo. When it came to avenging such wrongs and protecting their homeland, citizens of the fledgling Republic of Texas felt they had a right to take strong measures. But few of them acknowledged that Indians might have similar grounds for defying whites who infringed on tribal territory. One such confrontation occurred less than a month after San Jacinto, and it helped set Texans firmly against the Comanche and their tribal allies.

On the morning of May 19, a large party of mounted Indians approached a stockade in east Texas known as Parker's Fort, whose log walls enclosed the cabins of founder John Parker and other families who had joined him in this frontier outpost of about 30 people. The grim drama that followed would be reenacted many times in one form or another in years to come, but never with such powerful and surprising twists of fate.

The Parkers, emigrants from Virginia, were among some 30,000 Anglo-Americans who had settled in Texas since Mexico severed ties with Spain in 1821. The Mexican government had encouraged such settlement in its northern province with land grants in the hope that these pioneers would provide a buffer against continuing Comanche and Kiowa raids into south Texas and across the Rio Grande. But the newcomers settled initially along the rich river bottoms of southeast Texas, well away from the Comanchería and the path of the raiders. The settlers soon grew dissatisfied with Mexican rule, but they remained on fairly good terms with tribes of the region. By the time Texas achieved independence, however, relations between the Anglos and the Indians had begun to sour. Land-hungry farmers like the Parkers were moving out onto the fertile fringes of the Plains, kindling tribal resentment there.

Parker's Fort was located along a branch of the Brazos River, some 40 miles east of present-day Waco—a town named for a group of Wichitas who had migrated south into the area along with members of another Wichita band, the Tawakoni, several decades before the Parkers intruded. Resentful Wichitas may have been behind the expedition that descended on Parker's Fort in May, but they brought with them a strong and diverse group of supporters, including some Caddos—longtime residents of east Texas—a few Kiowas, and a large number of Comanches, who figured prominently in the ensuing action.

As the warriors neared the fort, one of them waved a white flag of truce affixed to the point of his lance. John Parker's grown son Benjamin walked out warily to greet the visitors. Through sign language and pidgin English, the Indians indicated that they were looking for a good camping place. They also said they were hungry and wanted a beef cow.

Benjamin returned to the stockade to report on the parley and express his opinion that the Indians were hostile. Over the protests of his family, he then went back outside to try to placate the visitors. He did not offer them food. Like other Anglo-Texans, the Parkers were reluctant to buy peace from Indians with gifts or tribute. As his relatives looked on in horror, Benjamin Parker was engulfed by warriors, who thrust their lances into him. Then the men stormed the stockade gate. Benjamin's brother Silas tried to bar the gate, but the warriors struck him down and raced inside the one-acre enclosure. In the ensuing melee, the attackers killed John Parker and four other men and mortally injured two women before riding off with five captives—two women and three young children.

The captives endured rough treatment in the days to come. Even the children were thrashed and taunted at first. And the two women, Elizabeth Kellogg and Rachel Parker Plummer, were raped and later entrusted to separate parties, who dealt with them harshly. Such abuse reflected the Indians' conviction that enemy women and children were as much to be scorned as enemy men and deserved no sympathy until they had been inducted into the tribe. After the initial ordeal, most captives were adopted by members of the tribe as sons or daughters, or taken as wives, and treated well. Some prisoners remained in a state of subservience, however, until their freedom was purchased. Elizabeth Kellogg was ransomed from Caddos after six months, and Rachel Plummer from Comanches after 18 months.

Rachel Plummer's account of her ordeal among the Comanches, published shortly after her release, incensed many Texans. And the anger only mounted as more white women and children were seized by Indians during clashes in the years to come and the tales of captivity proliferated. Many of the accounts were highly embellished and served to inflame passions against the Comanche and their allies, fueling demands for revenge.

One fact that was often overlooked in the furor was that white children taken by the Indians often heartily embraced native culture. All three youngsters captured during the attack on Parker's Fort became full-fledged members of Comanche society. Two of them, James Plummer and young John Parker, were ransomed six years after the raid, but Parker refused to adapt to white society and lived as a recluse. His sister Cynthia Ann, who was nine years old at the time of her capture and spent nearly a quarter-century among Comanches, had the strangest destiny of all. She grew up to become the wife of one chief and the mother of another, the celebrated Quanah Parker, who emerged as principal leader of the Comanche during their painful transition to reservation life. The raid on Parker's Fort did much to sow hatred and violence. But it also produced this unforeseen blessing—a chief who had the rare power to heal old wounds and mend broken spirits.

Not all whites in Texas regarded attacks like the one at Parker's Fort as grounds for waging war on Indians. One powerful and persistent advocate of peace was the first president of the republic, Sam Houston. As leader of the successful rebellion against the Mexicans, Houston was no pacifist, but he was sympathetic to the Indian cause. He had lived among Cherokees for three years in the Southeast and had perceived the culpability of whites. Nothing in Houston's experience, however, quite prepared him for

Known as Big Blond, or Kiowa Dutch, this son of German immigrants was adopted by Kiowas as a boy in 1835 and was still with the tribe when this picture was taken some 60 years later. Youngsters seized by Indians on the southern Plains often were treated harshly at first, but nearly all were adopted and became full members of the tribe.

the daunting task of reconciling proud Texans with the powerful Comanche, who dominated the southern Plains and exercised considerable influence over smaller, allied tribes such as the Kiowa and Wichita.

Although Houston negotiated at length with Comanche chiefs, he lacked the power to grant them what they wanted in return for a peace pledge—protection of their traditional hunting grounds. Chief Muguara of the Penateka, the southernmost Comanche division, said that whites would be left unharmed if "they would just draw a line showing what land they claim, and then keep on their side of it." Such a concession would have been anathema to Texans—who wanted to travel freely and settle where they pleased—and Houston admitted as much. "If I could build a wall from the Red River to the Rio Grande," he said, "the white people would go crazy and try to devise a means to get beyond it."

Large parts of the Comanchería consisted of semiarid grasslands, unsuitable for farming. But there were fertile areas at the eastern edges of the tribe's domain and along the region's rivers, and Texans coveted those spots. Over President Houston's veto, the legislature threw open the entire republic to settlement. Surveyors and land hunters responded by venturing beyond the existing frontier of settlement—a line extending north from San Antonio to the vicinity of present-day Dallas—and staking out homesteads for thousands of new emigrants lured to the republic by an offer of 1,280 free acres to every family. Comanches and Kiowas defended their territory, attacking the surveyors and the settlers who followed.

The fighting only intensified when Houston, at the end of his two-year term, was succeeded by Mirabeau B. Lamar in late 1838. Insisting that "the white man and the red man cannot dwell in harmony together," Lamar called for war on the Comanche and their allies "without mitigation or compassion." With broad popular support, Lamar persuaded the legislature to appropriate $1 million to build a system of frontier forts and raise 1,000 regular troops to fight Indians.

Lamar already had a fighting force at his disposal—companies of irregulars who gained lasting fame as the Texas Rangers. The name *ranger* went back to the 1820s, when Stephen F. Austin, leader of the first Anglo-American colonizers, applied it to the militiamen who clashed occasionally with Tonkawas and other tribal groups raiding for horses in east Texas. In the early days, local communities recruited and supported those irregulars. During the recent war for independence, however, Texas had authorized formation of ranging companies to protect settlers along the advancing frontier from Indian attacks. After the war such companies continued

Comanches on horseback clash with a wagon train of white settlers firing from the woods at left in this scene painted by George Catlin in 1847, a time when such conflict was rampant in Texas. Incited by white encroachment, Comanches and Kiowas attacked settlers at home and on the trail, prompting retaliation by mounted bands of Texas Rangers.

to operate in the name of the republic, which provided them with little or no pay and limited support in the form of equipment. The Rangers—typically young, footloose adventurers—often provided their own gear and even stole chickens or hogs to sustain themselves.

At first Rangers proved no match for the swift-riding Comanches. Taking cues from their foes, however, the Texans worked hard at acquiring equestrian skills and helped develop a new breed of war-horse that combined the speed and endurance of Indian ponies with the size and

strength of horses imported from the East. They also adopted the guerrilla tactics of their adversaries: riding silently by moonlight and surprising the enemy with attacks at daybreak. Ranger captains learned to locate hidden camps by following the vultures that fed on the entrails of animals cut up by Comanches. The Texans grew so adept at pursuing them, in fact, that the Comanches called them "those who always follow our trails."

Proof of the Rangers' growing capacity to inflict punishment came in the summer of 1839. Agents from Mexico, still hoping to drive the Anglo-Americans from Texas, were agitating among Cherokees who, after being displaced from their southeastern homeland, had emigrated to eastern Texas while others of their tribe settled to the north. Although Cherokees had lived in peace with Texans for 20 years and showed no inclination to turn against them now, Lamar unleashed his Rangers. In a quick and brutal campaign, they swept through Indian villages in east Texas, killing and burning out Cherokees and members of other displaced tribes from the East, including Creeks, Shawnees, and Kickapoos.

To deal similar blows to Comanches, who mounted up when challenged and fought from horseback, the Rangers required better weapons. The gun many Texans brought with them from the East, the Kentucky long rifle, was of little use to horsemen unless they first dismounted. The Rangers soon found what they needed for mounted warfare—pistols with revolving cylinders that held several bullets. The early models turned out by Samuel Colt were difficult to reload. But the celebrated Colt six-shooter gave a single Texas Ranger the firepower of a half-dozen men and allowed him to reply to the Comanche archer missile for missile.

A young Ranger captain named John Hays first realized the potential of Colt's pistol. Early in 1840 he was leading a detachment of 14 men armed with revolvers on a patrol along the Pedernales River, northwest of San Antonio, when they were challenged by some 70 Penateka Comanches intent on resisting

Sam Houston, first president of the Republic of Texas, believed in the right of Indians to retain their ancestral lands. During his two terms of office, he met with Comanche leaders several times, hoping to forge a lasting peace, but was unable to offer them guarantees against further encroachment.

Texas Rangers gained an edge over their Indian opponents with handy revolving pistols like this rare Colt five-shooter, manufactured in 1838.

this intrusion on their homeland. In such situations in the past, Rangers had raced for cover, dismounted, and fired their long rifles. This time, Hays's men remained in the saddle and met the Comanches with six-shooters blazing, killing 30 of them and scattering the rest. A few days later, in the Nueces Canyon west of San Antonio, the Rangers again used their revolvers to repulse a large force of Penatekas, inflicting many casualties and adding to the fearsome reputation of the new weapon among Comanche warriors. Soon Rangers acquired an even deadlier pistol—the Walker revolver, a long-barreled, easily loaded model named for Ranger Samuel Walker, who went east to help Colt perfect his six-shooter.

Patrols by well-armed Texas Rangers were only part of a larger problem facing the Penateka. Their rugged homeland, with its hills and canyons, was not all good buffalo country. Although bison remained an important resource for them, these so-called Honey Eaters filled out their diet by gathering nectar and stalking deer in lush wooded areas along rivers and streams. Those were the same inviting spots coveted by white settlers, and Penatekas had been mounting attacks on the intruders to fend them off. If the warriors lost control of their foraging grounds, Penatekas faced deprivation. Mindful of that fact, a number of their chiefs decided to seek a truce. In March 1840 a delegation consisting of Chief Muguara, 11 other leaders, and 52 warriors, women, and children traveled to San Antonio to meet with representatives of the Republic of Texas at the town's one-story courthouse, known thereafter as the Council House.

The Penatekas were not expecting violence. To Comanches, a council was sacred, and any act of hostility that marred the occasion was a sacrilege. Texas officials anticipated trouble, however, and were more than prepared for it. They ordered three companies of Texas regulars to stand by outside the courthouse.

As a condition for negotiations and proof of good intentions, the Texans had demanded that the Penatekas bring with them all the white captives held in their camps. The chiefs opened the council by handing over

just two captives—a little Mexican boy and a 16-year-old Texas girl, Matilda Lockhart. The girl's release only served to heighten tensions. Like the
two women taken at Parker's Fort, she had not been accepted quickly into
the tribe but had been treated as an enemy for some time. Her body and
face bore scars from punishment inflicted by her captors. Texans at the
council were alarmed by Matilda's condition and by her report that at least
15 more captives were being held by Penatekas. The angry delegates
asked the Comanches why the other captives had not been released.
Muguara, acting as spokesman, explained that they were being held by
bands over which he had no authority. He added that by tribal custom captives belonged to the individual warriors who had taken them. Some had
been adopted. But Muguara suggested that all of them could probably be
ransomed, one at a time, for the right price.

The Texans were in no mood to bargain. Officers rashly ordered soldiers into the Council House and instructed the interpreter to tell Muguara
that he and the other chiefs would be held hostage until every white captive held by the Penateka was released. At first the interpreter balked. He
knew the Comanches, and he warned that the chiefs would fight rather
than surrender. When the officer insisted, the interpreter translated the ultimatum and dashed out of the room, fearing for his life.

The Comanches jumped to their feet, shouting war cries. One chief
bolted for the door and stabbed a soldier barring his way. The troops
opened fire, and amid the smoke and confusion, Comanches and Texans
went down. Muguara drew a knife and stabbed an officer, only to be shot
dead by a soldier moments later. A few chiefs made it out into the court-
yard, where their families waited anxiously, hemmed in by soldiers. Out-
raged, Comanche men, women, and children lashed out at any Texans
within sight, including townspeople who had gathered around out of
curiosity. One Comanche youth wielded a small bow and fired an arrow
that struck a circuit judge in the heart, killing him instantly. Soon the surrounding troops opened fire, and the melee turned into a massacre. Fully
half of the Comanches were killed. The survivors were taken prisoner.

Others would suffer as well because of the disastrous decision to vio-
late the sanctity of the peace council and treat the chiefs as hostages. Hoping to salvage something from the debacle, Texans released the widow of
a Comanche chief and sent her home with a message for her people. Return the captives, they warned, or the Comanches languishing in the San
Antonio jail would be put to death. Unfortunately the Penateka no longer
trusted what the Texans said, and relatives of those killed at the Council

House yearned to atone for their losses. Grieving Comanche women first subjected themselves to intense pain by cutting off fingers or slashing themselves with knives. Then they rounded up most of the women and children being held captive, including Matilda Lockhart's six-year-old sister, and tortured them to death. Two captive children survived under the protection of those who had adopted them. Once the Texans in San Antonio learned there was nothing to be gained by holding the Comanches captive, some were let go and others were bound over in servitude to families in town, only to escape at the first opportunity and rejoin their people.

Efforts by Comanche warriors to reply to the Council House affront were at first disorganized. Soon afterward, several hundred men rode to San Antonio bent on revenge. But they were leaderless after the massacre, and most ended up milling around outside town in confusion, while a few warriors rode into San Antonio and shouted insults at the startled townspeople. Meanwhile, Muguara's nephew, known to whites as Buffalo Hump, was pondering a more cogent response. A staunch traditionalist who disdained the European clothing favored by many warriors, Buffalo Hump wore little more than a buffalo hide, wrapped around his hips. Intent on avenging his uncle and others slain at the Council House, he withdrew to a hilltop and sought a vision to guide him. In a moment of inspiration, he saw Texans being driven into the sea.

Lured by that prospect, Buffalo Hump assembled a huge party of Penatekas, including approximately 400 warriors and 600 women and children, and led them southeastward to the Gulf of Mexico. On August 6, they struck the town of Victoria, north of Corpus Christi, killing 15 people and making off with 2,000 head of livestock. Then they continued on to the sea, storming into Linnville, a tiny port on Lavaca Bay. All but five of the residents escaped by fleeing in boats moored in the harbor, and the raiders turned to looting a warehouse filled with bolts of cloth, stovepipe hats, and ladies' finery. Then they set the buildings afire and chased down stray cattle in the streets, lancing them as if they were buffalo.

Having driven some Texans into the sea, Buffalo Hump and his warriors prepared to return with their booty to their home encampments, some 300 miles away. Ordinarily Comanches who had ventured this deep into enemy territory would split up into small bands and take various trails to confuse pursuers. But Buffalo Hump chose to keep everyone together and trust in their combined numbers to protect the large herd of stolen horses and the heavily laden mule train. As the ponderous caravan moved northwestward, small detachments of Texans harassed the rear.

Up ahead, on a tributary of the San Marcos River called Plum Creek, waited a larger force of some 200 Texas Rangers, militiamen, and volunteers, along with 14 Tonkawa scouts so eager to get at their Comanche rivals that they had traveled 30 miles on foot. The Texans were surprised and pleased to see that only a small number of warriors rode as a screen for the huge column; the rest were dispersed throughout the procession, managing the horse herd and driving the mules. When the Comanche outriders caught sight of the waiting Texans, they put on a dazzling display, hoping to intimidate the enemy and protect the column. "It was a spectacle never to be forgotten," wrote John Holland Jenkins, a volunteer from the town of Bastrop. "Red ribbons streamed out from their horses' tails as they swept around us. There was a huge warrior, who wore a stovepipe hat, and another who wore a fine pigeon-tailed cloth coat, buttoned up behind. They bounded over the space between the hostile lines, exhibiting feats of horsemanship and daring."

Comanche warriors carried deerskin pouches such as the one above, which is adorned with trade beads. The pouches contained shot for the warriors' guns or sacred charms like eagle feathers.

The show delayed the Texans only momentarily. A Comanche warrior pranced out in front to exhibit his prowess and challenge the enemy. But a soldier in the distance gunned him down unceremoniously. Then the Texans charged, shooting the skirmishers and pressing in on the column from

Photographed in 1872 wearing the breastplate of the tribe's warriors, this Comanche bore the name of his father, Buffalo Hump, who battled Texans at Plum Creek.

either side. The uproar stampeded the horse herd just as the mule train ahead bogged down in wet ground. The swirling mass of horses and mules trapped many warriors, who were trampled—or shot by their assailants firing from the fringes of the pileup. The battle dissolved into a series of individual encounters. Fleeing Comanches abandoned their loot and began killing captives taken in the raid. One warrior tied a Texas woman to a tree and fired an arrow into her breast, but she survived because her whalebone corset blunted its force. The Texans responded in kind: John Jenkins saw a Ranger kick a dying Comanche woman and run her through with a lance.

Buffalo Hump and the other surviving Penatekas withdrew far into their country, and Texans went after them. In September President Lamar dispatched 90 Rangers and 12 Lipan Apache scouts—who, like the Tonkawas, had old scores to settle with Comanches—on a punitive expedition. Deep in the Comanchería, some 250 miles northwest of Austin, Colonel John Moore and his men located a Penateka encampment on a bend of the Colorado. Feeling secure in their tribal homeland, the Comanches had posted no sentinels, and the Texans surprised the inhabitants by attacking at first light on horseback. They shot up the camp, making no distinction between warriors and noncombatants, and then dismounted and picked off survivors attempting to escape across the river. "The bodies of men, women, and children were to be seen on every hand wounded, dying, and dead," reported Colonel Moore.

Devastated by the recent setbacks, most of the Penatekas retreated so far north that even the republic's peace emissaries had trouble finding them. Those emissaries were dispatched by Sam Houston, who was elected again to the presidency to succeed Lamar in 1841 and promptly cut off what little support the republic had provided for the Rangers and renewed efforts to achieve peace with the Indians. He wanted to bring all the chiefs together for a peace council. But messengers searched in vain for the main Penateka encampments.

Finally, in August 1843, a delegation found the camp of Pahayuco, a prominent Penateka civil chief. He and his people had moved far beyond the republic's borders, to the Canadian River in present-day Oklahoma. The Texans, carrying a flag of truce, invited the chief to Houston's peace council. But people in the camp remembered the Council House and de-

Chief Buffalo Hump's warriors—including one horseman sporting a top hat and an umbrella taken during a raid—collide with well-armed Texans at Plum Creek in August 1840. The Comanches were overwhelmed, losing 80 men and most of their booty.

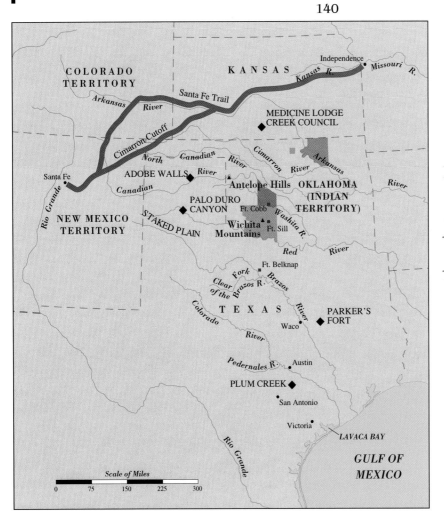

During the 19th century, Indians of the southern Plains lost nearly all their territory to Anglo-Americans. By 1880 tribes that once occupied parts of Texas had been driven from that state and relegated to reservations in Oklahoma—one in the southwest for Comanches, Kiowas, and Kiowa Apaches (orange); another nearby for Wichitas and Caddos (purple); and a small area up north for Tonkawas (green). Osages occupied a reservation in northeastern Oklahoma (pink) after losing the area that had been set aside for them in southern Kansas.

nounced them. Pahayuco convened a council to decide what to do with the emissaries. While the Texans waited nervously, warrior after warrior angrily called for them to be put to death, pointing out that a flag of truce had not helped the Comanches slain in San Antonio. But Pahayuco argued forcefully that nothing the Texans had done relieved Comanches of their traditional obligation to protect envoys who approached in peace. His prestige and eloquence carried the day, and the Texans were spared.

The following year, Houston finally managed to convene a peace council, at Tehuacana Creek, a tributary of the Brazos River. In attendance were Buffalo Hump and other Penateka leaders, as well as chiefs from some neighboring Wichita and Caddo bands. Houston blamed the rupture of peace on "a bad chief"—his predecessor, Lamar—and promised "to take away the blood from the path of the Comanche and the white people." He proposed establishing a boundary line through central Texas that whites could not cross without official permission. In fact he had no authority to enforce such a barrier and little chance of obtaining it from the legislature. But the matter was never put to a test. Comanches objected to the proposed line because it cut through their ancestral territory and limited their hunting range. As the old warrior Buffalo Hump remarked, the boundary was "too far up the country." Setting aside this stubborn problem, the two sides agreed to establish trading posts and offered mutual vows of friendship that included a Comanche pledge not to plunder Texas settlements.

Many Comanche chiefs were absent from this council, and their followers ignored its provisions. Even chiefs who attended, such as Buffalo Hump, felt free to continue raiding into Mexico—an activity that had become an important form of subsistence for southern Comanches as they lost their old hunting grounds. After his meeting with Sam Houston, Buffalo Hump rode into San Antonio and announced that the bad blood of the Council House had been "washed away by the water of peace." Officials there did nothing to dissuade him or other war chiefs from heading south into Mexico. On one occasion, officials even provided supplies to Comanche raiders bound for the Rio Grande. Encouraging such forays did not immunize Texans from attack, however. Inevitably raiders traveling to and from Mexico along Comanche trails west of the Texas frontier strayed and plundered exposed settlements.

In 1845 Texans voted overwhelmingly for annexation by the United States. When the republic officially became a state the following year, the federal government took over frontier defense. Federal authorities had been dealing with northern Comanche bands for many years, and officials met in April with a large delegation of Penatekas at Tehuacana Creek in the hope of arranging a peace treaty. The Penatekas were eager for a deal and promised to surrender captives, return stolen horses, and acknowledge the jurisdiction of the United States. There could be no peace without a secure homeland for the Comanche, however, and the federal government was powerless to offer any guarantee. All public land in Texas remained under the authority of the state. The reluctance of state officials to place any limits on settlement ensured that encroachment on the tribal domain would continue, along with raids and reprisals by Comanches.

The war that broke out between the United States and Mexico in 1846 diverted federal troops, and defense of the frontier fell to a revived regiment of Texas Rangers, commanded by John Hays. Once the Mexican War ended in 1848, however, the United States began constructing forts to keep peace along the Texas frontier. A chain of primitive outposts extended from the site of present-day Fort Worth southward through San Antonio to the Rio Grande. In theory the small garrisons of infantry assigned to the forts along this cordon were supposed to keep Texans and Comanches safely apart and prevent the Indians from raiding into Mexico, as specified by the treaty concluding the Mexican War. But the troops were in no position to prevent

Texans from entering the Comanchería, and settlers pressed beyond the existing frontier in such numbers that in 1850 the army had to construct a new cordon 100 miles or so to the west. Nor did the presence of troops do much to inhibit Comanche raiders. The garrisons were under orders to engage Indians only if they were caught in the act of raiding. Penatekas had little fear of the bluecoats and often camped near the forts to fraternize. They traded horses and joined the troops in games and horse races. Amid these friendly diversions, northern Comanches sometimes bypassed the forts to plunder settlements in south Texas and Mexico.

Like the Penatekas, northern Comanches and Kiowas persisted in raiding not simply out of a desire for adventure or glory but because the hunting grounds that had long brought them plenty were being usurped. In recent years, more and more tribal groups from east of the Mississippi had migrated to the Indian Territory willingly or under duress. Most of them settled in what is now eastern Oklahoma, at the edge of the Plains, but hunting parties of Cherokees, Shawnees, and Delawares, among others, ventured boldly onto the Kiowa and Comanche domain, despite the risk of encountering war parties. As more hunters competed for the buffalo, the great herds began to diminish.

At the same time, the cession by Mexico to the United States of a vast area in the West—including the territories of New Mexico, Colorado, and California—brought emigrants and speculators streaming across the southern Plains. Thousands of fortune hunters drawn by the discovery of gold in California in 1848 traveled from Missouri to New Mexico and points west along the original Santa Fe Trail, which paralleled the Arkansas River through Kansas. Others who started out on that trail followed a shortcut from central Kansas to Santa Fe along the upper Cimarron River, slicing through the Comanche and Kiowa heartland. Whatever route they took, the travelers antagonized tribes by fouling water holes and disrupting buffalo migration patterns. For four years in a row beginning in 1849, painted robe calendars of the Kiowa bore a notation signifying "few or no bison." In these lean times, Comanches took to eating their horses and began demanding tolls from travelers on the trails.

The forty-niners' most destructive legacy was disease. A cholera epidemic evidently started along the Arkansas River in the spring of 1849 and quickly spread southward. Indians became infected from polluted water, discarded garments, and the shallow graves of stricken travelers. The epidemic hit Penateka Comanches hard because they were pressed closer together now than they had been before and the disease was communicated

CHARMS OF THE OSAGE

Osage jewelry, lovingly crafted and proudly worn, is merely beautiful to the outsider. To the Osage, the designs incised or stamped onto the finery relate to a world-view and kinship system that predates written history.

Metal jewelry was unknown among the Osage before they came in contact with Europeans, but it was quickly accepted and, with great creativity, melded into their ancient cultural framework. According to Osage legend, the world is made up of two great parts, the earth and the heavens. Symbolically the people were divided as well into two major groups: the Tsi-zhu, representing the sky, peace, and harmony; and the Hon-ga, representing the earth, warfare, and protection. Accordingly, the jewelry worn by the Osage reflects their affiliation with either major group. Geometric designs, stars, and animal symbols proclaim the owner's kinship with clans belonging to heaven or earth.

Ida Michelle, an Osage girl photographed at the Saint Louis World's Fair in 1904, poses in traditional clothing, including the large silver pins like the one shown inset. The earrings below are the typical ball-and-cone style worn by both men and women since the 1700s, sometimes 20 or more per ear.

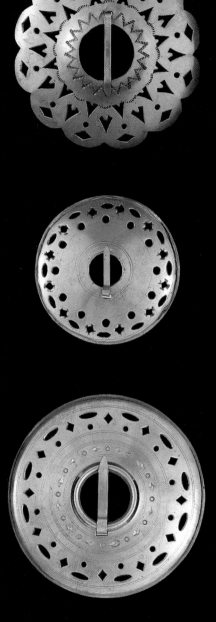

Four elaborately designed pins adorn the blouse of an Osage woman in this photograph taken about 1920. Large pins like those featured on this page were usually worn several at a time and only by female members of the tribe.

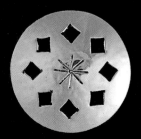

Roan Horse, an Osage man photographed about 1910, wears a neckerchief slide similar to the star-adorned example at lower right, signifying kinship in a celestial Tsi-zhu clan. The bear-paw slide at center right would proclaim affiliation with the Black Bear Clan of the Hon-ga.

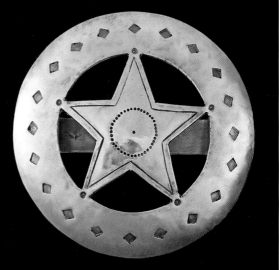

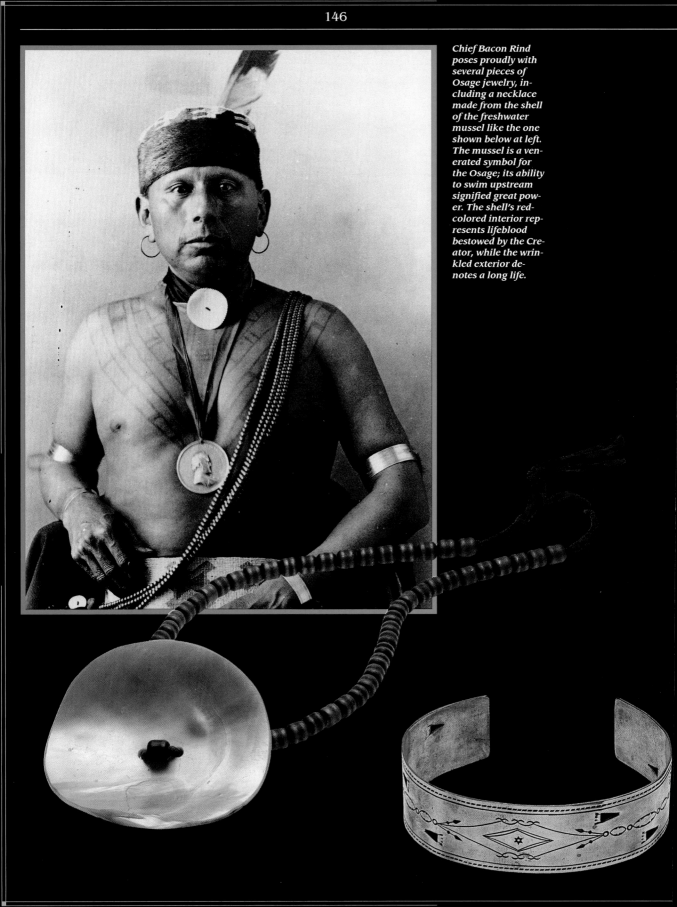

Chief Bacon Rind poses proudly with several pieces of Osage jewelry, including a necklace made from the shell of the freshwater mussel like the one shown below at left. The mussel is a venerated symbol for the Osage; its ability to swim upstream signified great power. The shell's red-colored interior represents lifeblood bestowed by the Creator, while the wrinkled exterior denotes a long life.

See-haw, a respected member of an Osage society known as the Little Old Men, wears his ceremonial best for a portrait made at the turn of the 20th century. Armbands crafted of German silver, such as the ones shown below, were embellished with otter fur on ceremonial occasions.

readily from camp to camp. In just a few months, up to half the Penatekas were wiped out. Many bands of Comanches and Kiowas to the north
suffered almost as severely. Shamans died even as they administered
herbs, chanted medicine songs, and tried other ancient remedies. Probably only the Comanche custom of fleeing an infected camp and never returning to a place where someone had died prevented their virtual extinction.

For the survivors, raiding the increasing numbers of white intruders
was often more rewarding than pursuing the diminishing herds of buffalo.
Far-ranging parties from north of the Red River supplanted the shrunken
bands of Penatekas as the principal threats to Texas and Mexico. The United States tried to contain these northern raiders through a treaty signed
by Kiowas and Yamparika Comanches at Fort Atkinson in Kansas in 1853.
But the agreement was largely ineffectual because it offered the Indians
little incentive to stop raiding. They received $18,000 a year in supplies,
but they were asked in return to put up with the construction of forts and
depots on their land and tolerate a continuing flow of emigrants that further disrupted their traditional subsistence patterns. Soon Comanches
and Kiowas were again exacting tolls from travelers on the Santa Fe Trail
and dispatching war parties southward. More than one official remarked
bitterly that Indians were attacking Texas settlers with arms and ammunition purchased with their Fort Atkinson annuities.

In Texas the plight of the surviving Penatekas and neighboring tribal
groups grew so desperate that state officials grudgingly agreed to create
two small reservations for them along the Brazos River and its tributary,
the Clear Fork, at the behest of federal Indian agents, who observed that
hunger was forcing even the proud Comanches to beg for food. One reservation was for Penatekas, the other for Wichitas and Caddos, along with a
few other small tribal factions. All of these groups had been greatly reduced by disease and deprivation as outsiders encroached on their homelands. Federal agents in charge of resettling the tribes could locate only
about 1,000 Penatekas and about 1,100 members of the other tribes—this
in a state that had been home to some 30,000 Indians a half-century before. Once spread out across a vast area, they were now asked to make do
with two tiny parcels of land totaling 56,000 acres. A Comanche chief by
the name of Shanaco protested to a federal agent: "You come into our
country and select a small patch of ground, around which you run a line,
and tell us the president will make us a present of this to live upon, when
everybody knows that the whole of the entire country, from the Red River
to the Colorado, is now and always has been ours."

Major Robert Neighbors, photographed with his wife in the 1850s, was one of a small number of white Texans who worked to protect Indians in the state. As a federal agent, he helped establish two small reserves in Texas for Caddos and southern Comanches. Later, when armed whites began to stalk the area, Neighbors conducted the endangered Indians to reservations in Oklahoma.

The Wichitas and Caddos adapted to reservation life fairly easily. A settled folk who had farmed part-time for centuries, they built thatch-roofed houses and planted corn. By contrast, fewer than half of the southern Comanches even reported to their reservation; the rest remained with Buffalo Hump and other chiefs camped beyond the frontier. Those who moved to the reservation made a stab at farming, and some of their children attended school there. But this was not the best land for cultivation, and men used to the pleasures and rewards of hunting and raiding found working the soil stultifying. Making a Comanche into a farmer, one chief protested, was like trying to turn a mighty wolf into a mere dog.

Buffalo Hump and other defiant kinsmen still living on the Plains stopped by the reservation occasionally to cadge coffee, sugar, and other supplies and invite warriors to join them on raids. Few yielded to that temptation, but Texans tended to blame the reservation dwellers for raids conducted by the holdouts or by northern bands. To make matters worse, both reservations were soon surrounded by settlers. Those fearful and angry neighbors formed vigilante groups that attacked, robbed, and killed Indians on and off the reservations. In one instance, Caddos aided by federal troops managed to repulse a mob of 250 settlers at their reservation.

The chief federal agent in Texas, Robert Neighbors, saw that something had to be done. A man of principle, Neighbors doubted the federal government could keep its commitment to protect the reservation dwellers in the face of mounting pressure, and he persuaded authorities to resettle them in safer environs—the western part of present-day Oklahoma. In the summer of 1859, Neighbors and four companies of soldiers escorted 1,112 Wichitas

and Caddos and 384 Comanches northward, marching them away from the reservations in such haste that much of their livestock had to be left behind. On September 1, when the procession forded the Red River into the Indian Territory, Neighbors wrote his wife of their exodus: "I have this day crossed all the Indians out of the heathen land of Texas and am now out of the land of the Philistines." As Neighbors made his way back through Texas after delivering his charges to Fort Cobb, he stopped in the village of Fort Belknap. A man he did not know, an Indian-hating, shotgun-toting Texan named Ed Cornett, blasted the agent in the back, killing him instantly.

During the same period, Texans began a campaign to scourge the Comanches who were still roaming free. In the spring of 1858, the state

A man sits atop a mound of some 40,000 buffalo hides at a rail yard in Dodge City, Kansas, in 1873. To keep Indian bands from roaming the Plains, the government encouraged professional hunters to slaughter the last great herds of buffalo, whose numbers had been diminishing since the late 1840s. According to General Philip Sheridan, killing the buffalo was "the only way to bring lasting peace and allow civilization to advance."

raised a new company of Rangers under the veteran Captain John "Rip" Ford and authorized him to "follow any and all trails of hostile or suspected hostile Indians" and inflict "summary punishment on them." With approximately 100 Rangers and an equal number of Indian scouts and auxiliaries from the Caddo reservation, Ford crossed the Red River and trespassed on federal land in Oklahoma. North of the Canadian River in the Antelope Hills—well beyond Ranger jurisdiction—his Indian scouts located the village of Iron Jacket, a prominent chief of the Kotsoteka Comanches, who had long resided in the area. Iron Jacket's name and reputation rested on a suit of armor he wore in battle. His coat of mail, a relic from a Spanish warrior of the previous century, was thought to render him invulnerable to arrows and rifle balls alike.

Captain Ford's men confronted Iron Jacket's warriors near their village. The chief, resplendent in his armor and a headdress studded with feathers and long red streamers, rode between the opposing lines with his lance, challenging the enemy. In the opening volley, Iron Jacket went down, killed by a single shot. Ford then gave the order to charge, and his men routed the Comanches, claiming 76 lives.

Far from attempting to prevent such unauthorized incursions by Texas troops onto federal territory, the U.S. Army tried to outdo the Rangers in punishing Comanches. Since 1855 the 2nd Cavalry Regiment—whose officer corps included such future heroes of the Civil War as John Bell Hood and Robert E. Lee—had been patrolling the open spaces between forts on the Texas frontier in the hope of discouraging Indian raids. Now, prodded by Texas authorities and spurred by Ford's raid, the 2nd Cavalry sought permission to launch an offensive. In the late summer of 1858, Major Earl Van Dorn led four companies of cavalry, 50 infantrymen, and 135 Indian auxiliaries north across the Red River into Oklahoma. Near Rush Springs they found the camp of Buffalo Hump and attacked at dawn, firing indiscriminately into the lodges. More than 50 Comanches were killed, but old Buffalo Hump led many others to safety in a nearby ravine while his warriors fought back, wounding Van Dorn and killing several of his men.

Van Dorn recovered and relentlessly pursued Buffalo Hump, who withdrew northward into Kansas. The following May, Van Dorn's cavalry struck again, assaulting the chief's camp near the Arkansas River while many of the warriors were away hunting. The federal troops killed, wounded, or captured most of the 100 or so Comanche men, women, and children gathered there and forced the rest to abandon their belongings. Although Buffalo Hump eluded capture, he and the remaining holdouts later joined

WOHAW

the survivors of the attack on the Comanche reservation in Oklahoma.

By 1860, the eve of the Civil War, the Comanche and their tribal allies were in disarray. Many bands were discouraged, decimated by disease, and hungry. Indians had been deprived of their last enclaves in the settled parts of Texas and could be shot on sight as outlaws anywhere in the state. Some 500 Texas Rangers roamed the frontier, along with local volunteers known as minutemen. The 2nd Cavalry Regiment and other federal units in Texas numbering 2,500 men continued their relentless patrols. No longer could war parties range undisturbed across the southern Plains.

The fate of one group of raiders underscored how much Comanche power had diminished since the attack on Parker's Fort nearly 25 years earlier. In the fall of 1860, Chief Peta Nocone organized a raiding party among his followers, the Nokoni—an elusive division of Comanches who had once dominated east-central Texas, north of the Penateka, but had recently taken refuge up near the Texas Panhandle, which had yet to be claimed by whites. Nocone and his raiders eluded patrols and traveled to

The abrupt transition of southern Plains Indians to reservation life is depicted in this drawing done in 1877 by the Kiowa artist Wohaw, which shows a buffalo beside a tipi on the open Plains at left and a steer next to a frame house on a reservation at right. Wohaw stands at the center of the drawing, extending peace pipes toward both animals but facing the steer, perhaps signifying his acceptance of the new way of life.

the Waco area and beyond, passing near the site of Parker's Fort, before encountering resistance and turning back. As they headed home, they were tracked and pursued by a combined force of some 150 Rangers, federal cavalrymen, and local volunteers under Captain L. S. Ross. In December Ross and his men finally caught up with the Comanches, camped along the Pease River, west of Wichita Falls. Attacking amid swirling dust whipped up by a northerly gale, Ross gunned down a man he believed to be Chief Nocone. Other accounts indicate that Nocone survived, however, and died the following year of a wound sustained elsewhere. In fact nearly all the warriors were off hunting when Ross struck, and those killed or taken prisoner during the assault were mostly women and children.

Among the captives was Nocone's wife—a white woman with blue eyes—and the couple's infant daughter. The woman called herself Naduah, but Ross thought he knew her original identity. He took her to see Colonel Isaac Parker, uncle of the girl who had been taken from Parker's Fort in 1836. The colonel did not at first recognize this woman, who understood no English. But when he spoke the name Cynthia Ann, she broke into tears.

Reunited with relatives, Cynthia Ann Parker, now 34, learned the English language anew and did her best to adapt in other ways. On one occasion, however, she plotted unsuccessfully to return to the Comanchería so she could be with her two sons. And after her daughter, Prairie Flower, died of smallpox in 1864, she grieved as a true Comanche, mutilating herself and refusing to eat. Cynthia Ann Parker died in mourning a short time later—unaware that one of her children, the young man called Quanah, or Sweet Smell, had already won distinction among his own people and would soon command respect among whites as well.

After the tumult of the Civil War, settlers surged westward with fresh impetus. Even the semiarid grasslands were now being infringed on by cattle ranchers. In order to secure the advancing frontier, federal authorities launched a concerted effort to confine to reservations all tribal groups who were still roaming free. In 1867 chiefs of the Comanche, Kiowa, and other tribes of the southern Plains consented to meet with officials at Medicine Lodge Creek in Kansas. Among the 4,000 Indians attending this great council were Cheyennes and Arapahos from north of the Arkansas River who had kept peace with Comanches and Kiowas since 1840, when the two sides agreed to cease their feuding and accept the Arkansas as a boundary.

Many of the chiefs who came to the Medicine Lodge council along with their followers had already seen much of their territory stripped away and were reluctant to surrender any more land. A prominent spokesman for the Comanches, Ten Bears, a leader of the Yamparika, ended his address to the white treaty makers with a fervent plea: "That which you now say we must live on is too small. The Texans have taken away the places where the grass grew the thickest and the timber was the best. The white man has the country which we loved, and we only wish to wander on the prairie until we die."

The federal government had no intention of letting Comanches live out their lives as they pleased. Officials were there not to bargain with the Indians but to reconcile them to the fate that the government had decreed for them—confinement to small patches of the Indian Territory. The tract set aside for Comanches and Kiowas lay in the southwest corner of present-day Oklahoma. This 5,546-square-mile area—baldly expropriated from Choctaws and Chickasaws as punishment for their failure to support

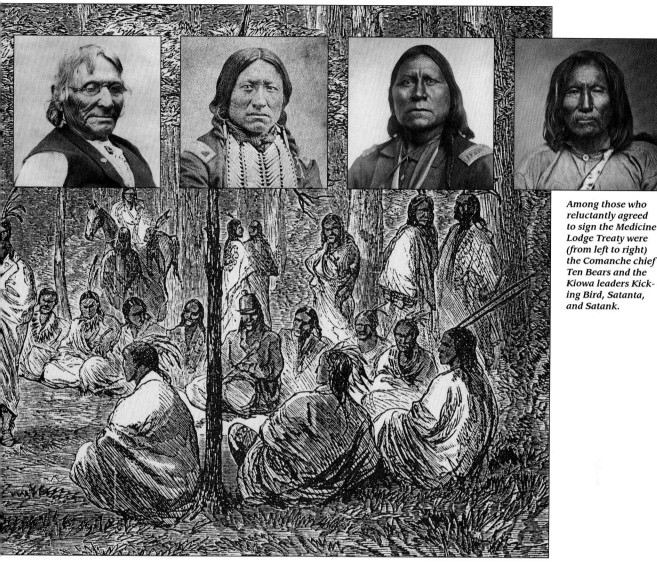

Among those who reluctantly agreed to sign the Medicine Lodge Treaty were (from left to right) the Comanche chief Ten Bears and the Kiowa leaders Kicking Bird, Satanta, and Satank.

Comanches, Kiowas, and delegates from other Plains tribes meet with U.S. negotiators during the great peace council held near Medicine Lodge Creek in Kansas in 1867. Gifts to the chiefs did little to ease the painful concessions they were asked to make—abandonment of their ancestral ways and confinement to reservations. "Why do you ask us to leave the rivers, and the sun, and the wind, and live in houses?" demanded the Comanche chief Ten Bears. "Do not ask us to give up the buffalo for the sheep."

the Union during the Civil War—represented only a tiny fraction of the Comanchería and excluded the best of the traditional hunting grounds.

The chiefs who signed the Medicine Lodge Treaty did so with heavy hearts, in the hope of avoiding a confrontation. Few had any intention of settling on the reservation, but they feared that rejecting the treaty outright would bring reprisals. The army's representative at the council, General William Tecumseh Sherman of Civil War fame, warned them pointedly: "You can no more stop this than you can stop the sun or moon; you must submit and do the best you can." The treaty signers represented only a portion of each tribe, but the United States considered the deal binding on all bands and claimed the right to force holdouts onto their allotted reservations at gunpoint.

After the council, only one tribe on the southern Plains retained an officially recognized homeland outside the Indian Territory—the Osage. Since 1825 they had clung to their reservation in southern Kansas despite incursions by whites and Indians alike. Although the land set aside for the

Osage was only a small portion of what they had once claimed, it was precious to them because it included good hunting grounds, where they stalked buffalo as of old. Like other tribes, they were promised their reservation for "as long as the grass grows and water flows." The grass was still growing and the water flowing, but that only made the area more attractive to settlers and their government sponsors. By 1869 more than 2,000 whites were squatting on Osage territory, and leaders of the tribe reluctantly agreed to a government proposal that they move south to the Indian Territory and settle on reservation land purchased from the Cherokee. Before the Osage departed, one journalist reported, the air was filled with the cries of old women, lamenting "over the graves of their children, which they were about to leave forever."

Elsewhere on the southern Plains, many tribal bands shunned the reservations. Following the Medicine Lodge council, only about one-third of the some 2,400 surviving Comanches moved to their assigned reservation. The rest forsook the canvas tipis, calico clothing, and government issue beef and continued to hunt and raid. The most determined holdouts were the westernmost division, the Quahada, who roamed the Staked Plain of western Texas and southeastern New Mexico. In that rugged and remote country, the Quahada had little contact with settlers and largely eluded punitive expeditions mounted by Texas Rangers and the U.S. Army. In recent years, the hard-riding Quahada had prospered by stealing cattle as well as horses from Texas ranches. Since they still obtained food by hunting buffalo and other game, they could afford to offer most of the livestock they corralled to the traveling New Mexico traders known as comancheros in exchange for necessities and luxuries, including ammunition, tobacco, and whiskey. If the corral was bare when a comanchero showed up at a Quahada camp, the warriors sometimes obliged by carrying out a quick raid for livestock while the buyer waited.

Among the leaders of these defiant Comanches was the young war chief Quanah Parker, who had been adopted by Quahadas following the capture of

The Comanche medicine man Ishatai, or Eschiti—shown seated amid family members at left—issued prophecies that inspired the ill-fated attack by Comanches, Kiowas, and Cheyennes on white buffalo hunters at Adobe Walls in the summer of 1874. Afterward members of the defiant bands tried to elude pursuing troops by hiding out in nearby Palo Duro Canyon (above) and other rugged spots along the upper Red River and tributaries.

his mother and the death of his father. Quanah had grown up to become a horseman and warrior of consummate skill and resolve, leading war parties up and down the Texas frontier. Cavalry patrols scouring the Plains gradually forced other Comanches—Yamparikas, Kotsotekas, and Nokonis—to move to the reservation, but Quanah and his Quahadas held out. They harassed the bluecoats, picking off sentries and stampeding horses before galloping off.

In 1874 the Quahada, inspired by the visions of a Comanche shaman named Eschiti, launched a desperate campaign to preserve their way of life. That spring, they met in council on the Red River with other defiant

Comanches, Kiowas, and Cheyennes. At Eschiti's urging, the Comanches joined in the Sun Dance—a ceremony that was new to them but offered inspiration in this time of peril. During the council, the Indians learned of the presence of commercial buffalo hunters at a trading post in the Texas Panhandle, built near the ruins of an old fort called Adobe Walls. It lay in prime buffalo country along the upper Canadian River, and the hunters there, armed with high-powered rifles, were systematically extinguishing the creatures who had brought the Comanche and their allies prosperity and power. The hunters cared only for the furs, which were shipped to factories for processing, and left the meat to rot. They were violating the terms of the Medicine Lodge Treaty, which gave the Indians exclusive hunting rights south of the Arkansas. But the army looked the other way, realizing as one general put it that the hunters were destroying the "commissary" that allowed Indians to survive outside the reservation.

Kiowa war chief Lone Wolf fought white hunters at Adobe Walls—and Texas Rangers afterward—in part to avenge the death of his son during a raid. He once vowed to make war on hostile Americans even if it meant annihilation for him and his people: "We are driven to it. We had rather die than live."

In June a war party consisting of several hundred men—including Quanah's Quahadas along with Kiowas and Cheyennes—set out for Adobe Walls. Their prospects appeared good. Only 28 hunters occupied the post. But when the Indians swooped down on them at dawn, the defenders were ready. From their sod houses, they trained on their assailants the same rifles that were destroying the buffalo herds. These .50-caliber weapons, with their telescopic sights, could pick off a target up to a mile away. But there was no need for long-range marksmanship. The attackers mounted charge after charge, presenting easy targets before swerving away as they neared the cabins. The bugle call of an Indian who borrowed his technique from cavalry trumpeters aided the defenders by alerting them to each new onslaught.

Quanah distinguished himself in battle as never before. He rode his horse right up to one of the cabins and tried to back through a barred door. Again and again he galloped through the sharpshooters' fire, one time dangling from his horse by an arm and foot to rescue a wounded comrade. Later his horse was shot from under him and he suffered a shoulder wound. But no amount of personal heroism could dislodge the buffalo hunters. The campaign, just begun, was over.

Crushed in spirit and facing new efforts by the army to attack their camps and force them onto the reservation, the warriors took refuge with women and children of their bands amid broken terrain in and around the Texas Panhandle. Nearly 5,000 Comanches, Kiowas, and Cheyennes sought sanctuary there in the canyons and arroyos carved by the headwaters of the Red River and its tributary, the Washita. But a half-dozen columns of cavalry and infantry converged on the Indians from all sides that summer and hounded them through the fall. A single raid on a Quahada camp in Palo Duro Canyon dealt a huge blow; the Comanches lost some 1,500 mounts in the strike. In all, the campaign, known as the Red River War, stripped the Indians of the means to survive away from the reservation. Soldiers probed relentlessly for their hiding places, burned their lodges, destroyed their winter provisions, and killed or confiscated more than 7,500 horses and mules.

Starving, freezing, and bereft of the mounts needed to hunt the scarce buffalo, a steady stream of Indians flowed onto the reservation, surrendering at Fort Sill, the new military post. Among the last to yield were Kiowas. Since the death in 1866 of their principal chief, Dohausen, who had favored peace, resolute war leaders had dominated tribal affairs. Some of these militants, including the influential chief Satanta, had signed the Medicine Lodge Treaty and even spent time on the reservation, but they never renounced the right to lead raids against their old enemies, the Texans, or to attack whites who intruded on Kiowa hunting grounds. War leaders like Lone Wolf swore that they would rather die fighting than yield to hostile authorities. But now concern for the fate of their followers induced them to surrender. In February 1875 Lone Wolf led his band to Fort Sill, marking the end of organized Kiowa resistance.

A small number of isolated bands from other tribes remained at liberty. In March of that year, some defiant Cheyennes straggled into the agency, arriving there "nearly starved to death, and in a deplorable condition," in the words of the commander. By late spring federal cavalrymen located the last of the holdouts—Chief Quanah and his band—and issued

Below, in a painting from 1890, Indians pursue cattle released from pens on a reservation in Oklahoma. As shown at right in a picture taken a few years later, women butchered the cattle as they once had the bison. But pursuing cattle was a poor substitute for the buffalo hunts of old.

Julian Scott

them an ultimatum: Submit or die. On June 2, 1875, Quanah and 406 of his people arrived at Fort Sill. Their surrender marked the end of hostilities—and of the long era of Comanche eminence on the southern Plains.

For the first time in history, the entire Comanche community was gathered in one small area. They were sadly reduced in number. According to one estimate, the Comanche population had stood at nearly 20,000 earlier in the century. Now only 1,600 remained. The federal government did little to rehabilitate the Comanche or their Kiowa neighbors. Food rations were small, and there were few buffalo to be had within the bounds of the reservation. Agents from the Bureau of Indian Affairs attempted to teach people about farming, but few reservation dwellers proved willing to learn, and those who gave it a try were frustrated by poor soil and dry weather. Efforts to introduce sheepherding and cattle ranching to the reservation met with similar resistance.

Longing for their old way of life, the Indians obtained official permission for a buffalo hunt off the reservation and were provided with a cavalry escort. For weeks practically the entire tribe scoured the Plains, making their way down into the Texas Panhandle and scouting every creek bed and water hole. They found not a single living buffalo, only bleached skulls and bones blanketing the grasslands where millions once grazed. By the end of the hunt in midwinter, game of any kind was so scarce that the people had to subsist on rations sent from the reservation and on 20 steers sold to them by a local rancher on credit.

Attempts by the government to transform the Indians culturally were largely unsuccessful. Frame houses stood empty while residents went

about their business from tipis pitched alongside. The Indian agency built boarding schools for the reservation children in the hope that separation from their families would hasten their assimilation. But many parents refused to send their children to these schools, believing that it was cruel to take children from their homes and subject them to a discipline that seemed harsh when compared with their traditional upbringing, which allowed youngsters considerable freedom.

Missionaries, for their part, sometimes found an eager audience among the reservation dwellers, who had always been curious about the medicine, or spirit powers, of other groups. When Christian preachers spoke in parables or metaphors, however, Comanches and Kiowas drew their own conclusions. Jim Whitewolf, a Kiowa Apache who grew up on the Oklahoma reservation in the 1880s, recalled that when a minister there promised Indians resurrection, they thought he was some kind of medicine man who could bring the dead back to life in the flesh. "Everybody started sending their children to that church," Whitewolf remembered. When it came to moral teachings, reservation dwellers obeyed those rules that agreed with their own traditions. Whitewolf recalled the reaction of an older Kiowa named Henry Brownbear when a missionary spelled out the Ten Commandments. Brownbear was willing to go along with the commandment against theft, for he had given up stealing horses. And he was happy to renounce lying, since he and his fellow Kiowas believed in speaking the truth. But Brownbear balked when the preacher said it was against God's law to long for another man's wife. "That's too much," Brownbear muttered. "I guess I'll just have to go to hell."

More persuasive than any outside teachers or preachers were leaders from within who urged the people to make the most of reservation life. No Comanche did more in that regard than Quanah, who had earned the right

Photographed in the early 1890s, the Comanche leader Quanah Parker stands on the porch of his home beside Tonasa, one of five wives then living with him at his imposing Oklahoma residence (top), known as the star house for the emblems on the roof. Quanah never relinquished his Comanche braids—or the practice of polygamy. When advised by whites to choose one wife and tell the others to leave, he replied sharply: "You come to my house. You pick out a wife for me to keep. Then you tell 'em."

Five of Quanah Parker's 25 children gather for a portrait in 1892, wearing a mix of traditional and contemporary clothing. To this day, Quanah's numerous descendants gather for a family reunion on the Fourth of July.

to promote peaceful accommodation by proving himself as a war leader. Not yet 30 years old when he surrendered, he dealt shrewdly and diplomatically with white officials. He retained fond memories of his white mother and formally took her surname. Late in life, after asking the governor of Texas to protect him from potential troublemakers, he journeyed to his mother's burial place in east Texas and brought her remains back to the reservation.

Although Comanches as a whole had no principal chief by tradition, Quanah's ability to deal with authorities made him recognized as such by whites and by most members of the tribe. In his capacity as leader, Quanah organized a movement among the Indians that forced surrounding ranchers to pay for grazing rights for their cattle, which had been trespassing on reservation lands. Although cattlemen paid only six cents an acre for the rights, leasing became the main source of revenue for reservation dwellers, who continued to resist farming or ranching themselves. By the mid-1890s nearly half the three-million-acre reservation was under lease, yielding total payments of $80,000 a year in so-called grass money to Comanches and Kiowas.

Comanche chiefs had long been men of wealth, and Quanah was no exception. He profited personally from the arrangement with the ranchers. For administering the leases, cattlemen put him on the monthly payroll and helped finance construction of a 12-room house, complete with a two-story porch, white picket fence, and stars emblazoned on the roof. In spite of his dealings with outsiders, Quanah refused to abandon Comanche customs: He wore his hair long in twin braids, wrapped himself in a blanket and buckskin for everyday business, and, much to the distress of government authorities, maintained up to a half-dozen wives.

He also adhered to a native form of spirituality by helping to establish among his people the peyote ritual. Comanches had known about peyote for some time and had probably collected peyote buttons for medicinal and other purposes during their forays into northern Mexico, where the plant grew profusely. But only on the reservation did it become the center of a religion that celebrated the ties of the people to the earth, moon, sun, and other transcendent powers. Those who traveled the Peyote Road, as the ritual was known, gained spiritual solace in a time of emotional trauma as well as a strong sense of community. Despite government attempts to ban the cult, it spread to other reservations, forming the basis for a formal religious denomination, the Native American Church.

The tribal solidarity fostered by leaders like Quanah was threatened when federal authorities set out to end communal ownership of reservations in Oklahoma and elsewhere, as decreed by the General Allotment Act of 1887. This measure, designed to assimilate Indians into the larger society and open tribal land for homesteading, assigned plots of 160 acres to heads of families and offered most of the remaining land to settlers. True to their traditions, Indians of the southern Plains resisted this assault on tribal territory—land that had been guaranteed to them in perpetuity. The Kiowa leader Lone Wolf, who received that honored name from the Kiowa war chief Lone Wolf, fought for his people in court, filing suit to block allotment as a violation of the Medicine Lodge Treaty. His case reached the Supreme Court, which ruled against him on the grounds that forcing Congress to honor past treaties jeopardized the government's role as guardian and protector of the Indians. This landmark ruling made little sense to the Kiowa and their tribal neighbors, who were being stripped of their collective inheritance by their "guardians" in Washington.

The Osage fought allotment by protesting that hundreds of those on the tribal rolls drawn up by the government were not entitled to land because they had little or no Osage ancestry. Such tactics delayed allotment long enough to enable the tribe to reap a major benefit. In 1894 oil was discovered on the reservation, and tribal leaders obtained an agreement that brought them 10 percent of the revenues. By the time the reservation was allotted in 1906, Osage families had benefited substantially from the oil lease and were in a better position to make the transition the government demanded of them.

The Comanche also delayed allotment and held out for better terms, including the right to retain 480,000 acres of communal property for lease to cattle ranchers. Six years later, they lost even that land, which the government sold off to homesteaders. By the time Quanah Parker died in 1911, the 1,500 or so Comanches were living as bands on a few small islands of land, each made up of adjacent allotments, amid a sea of more than 30,000 white settlers. But Quanah's memory lived on, as did the communal pride he helped rekindle among his people. His name is honored today, along with that of other tribal leaders and warriors, when far-flung Comanches gather in Oklahoma for their joyous homecomings—celebrations of a people who faced great challenges during their history and suffered many losses, yet emerged strong in spirit. ◆

Quanah Parker penned this letter to the governor of Texas in 1909 asking for official protection so that he could travel to Texas undisturbed and bring back to Oklahoma the remains of his mother. Quanah made the trip and laid his mother's bones to rest on the reservation. He was buried there beside her in 1911.

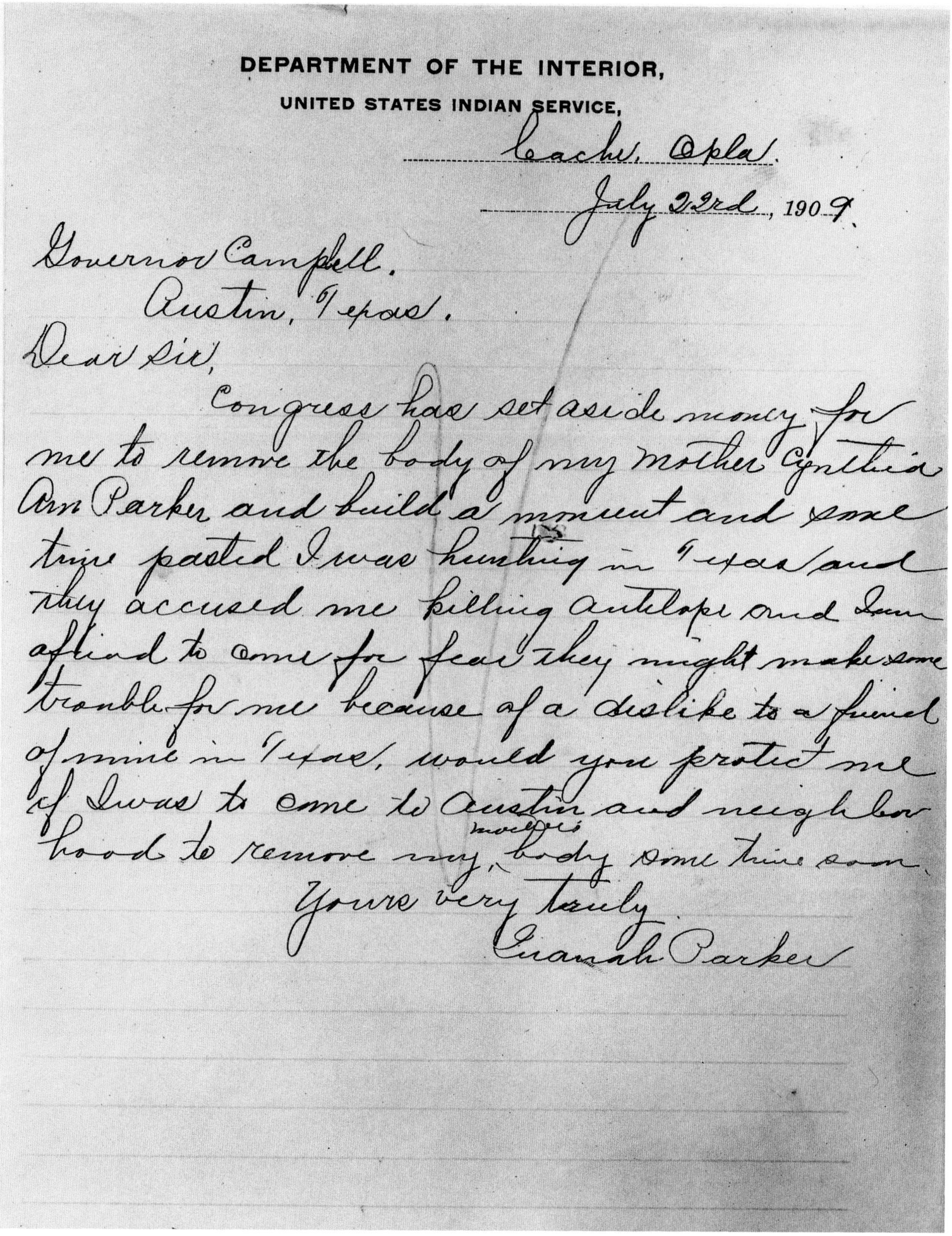

DEPARTMENT OF THE INTERIOR,

UNITED STATES INDIAN SERVICE,

Cache, Okla.

July 22rd, 1909.

Governor Campbell.

Austin, Texas.

Dear Sir,

Congress has set aside money for me to remove the body of my mother Cynthia Ann Parker and build a monument and some time pasted I was hunting in Texas and they accused me killing antelope and I am afraid to come for fear they might make some trouble for me because of a dislike to a friend of mine in Texas, would you protect me if I was to come to Austin and neighbor hood to remove my mothers body some time soon.

Yours very truly

Quanah Parker

FAIRS FOR A PROUD NATION

Each year the Nermernuh, as the Comanche people refer to themselves, hold two great powwows in southwestern Oklahoma, where about half of the estimated 9,000 tribal members reside. Both events—the Comanche Homecoming in July and the Comanche Nation Fair in October—are three-day campground gatherings featuring Comanche music, dancing, horse racing, games, storytelling, and other customs intrinsic to the people.

Moving to the tempo of an honoring song, Comanche dancers dressed in their ceremonial regalia head toward the arena to begin the dance programs at the 1993 Comanche Nation Fair at Camp Eagle, Oklahoma.

"There is a renaissance today of our traditions," says Comanche artist Walter Tutsi Wai BigBee. "The Comanche Homecoming and the Comanche Nation Fair provide a forum to celebrate, remember, and transmit those traditions to our young people, a place to gather and tell the world: 'We are still here. We have always been here.' "

A successful professional photographer, BigBee participates in the annual gatherings, focusing his lens on the activities and ceremonies. The pictures shown here are samples of his work. "I'm not a storyteller in the traditional sense," BigBee claims. "I can't speak Comanche. But with a camera, I can use a modern tool to help pass along traditions and innovations visually the way our oral historians have always done with their stories."

Carrying the lance and breastplate of a 19th-century Comanche warrior, a youthful dancer awaits the beginning of the Comanche Nation Fair parade. The hawk feathers in his hand denote a minor's status. The black stripe painted across his eyes is a personal insignia.

A TIME OF ANTICIPATION

Gourd Dancer Randy King prepares his dance regalia with the assistance of his wife and daughter. All the dancers take great care to ensure that their appearance reflects well on their families.

Members of the Little Ponies, a Gourd Dance society, begin the Brush Dance that will take them through the campgrounds and into the arena where the Gourd Dance program takes place. The Brush Dance serves as a notice to other Gourd Dancers to join in.

Morgan Tosee and his daughter Rachelle ride pinto ponies to the location where their group is assembling for the opening parade of the 1993 Comanche Nation Fair.

DANCES FOR THE WARRIORS

Honored military veterans wield traditional weapons and shields while performing the Tuh Wii, a dance that commemorates the deeds of a Comanche warrior from long ago. Lost since the reservation period, which ended in 1901, the dance was revived in 1975 and is now performed at significant Comanche gatherings.

Comanche War Scouts, a group of U.S. military veterans, perform in the esteemed lead position during the Grand Entry Dance. The Comanche have always honored men who served in the armed forces and following World War II created the annual Homecoming.

THE JOYS OF COMPETING

Sally Kerchee Hart performs in the regalia of a Comanche man (left), and men wearing women's attire step in time together during the Switch Dance competition, an often bawdy exchange of gender roles. The Switch Dance brings welcome comic relief to the lengthy dance programs.

Riders thunder by on their mounts during one of several horse races that are held during the gatherings. The races commemorate the Comanche tradition of superior horsemanship and are open to all comers, who compete for prizes and honor.

A Comanche woman prepares dough for the fry-bread contest. Accomplished fry-bread makers have their own unique methods and are held in high esteem by the community. They are often asked to cook for special events.

EVENING'S FESTIVITIES

A family gives away blankets, shawls, and other useful items, including money, to honor a close relative during a Giveaway Special at the 1994 Comanche Homecoming. The ceremony is in keeping with the Plains custom of sharing wealth in the community.

Hand game players (right and below) enjoy raucous competitions at most Comanche gatherings. Two bones, one marked and one unmarked, are used in this ancient game. Choosers from one team try to guess in which hand the other team's hider has placed the marked bone. Wagering can be heavy, and opposing teams constantly attempt to distract each other by beating drums, shaking rattles, and singing taunting songs.

AN ALL-EMBRACING FINISH

A group of tradition-al dancers look to-ward the arena as the night's competi-tion winds down. Dancers are judged in a number of cate-gories, and their elaborate feather bustles accent the intricate steps.

Comanches of all ages joyfully two-step around the arena during the social dance that follows a night's competition. No regalia or special skills are required for this part of the gathering, and everyone is welcome to participate. The celebration frequently continues until the wee hours of the morning.

ACKNOWLEDGMENTS

The editors wish to thank the following individuals and institutions for their valuable assistance:

In Denmark:
Copenhagen—Berete Due, Department of Ethnography, The National Museum of Denmark.

In the United States:
Arizona: Phoenix—Richard Pearce-Moses, The Heard Museum.
Illinois: Chicago—Nina Cummings, Field Museum; Michelle J. Dorgan, Special Collections, Newberry Library.
Missouri: St. Louis—Deborah Brown, Duane Sneddeker, Missouri Historical Society.
Oklahoma: Fort Sill—Towana D. Spivey, Fort Sill Museum. Lawton—Wallace Caffey, Comanche Tribe. Norman—Julie Droke, Oklahoma Museum of Natural History, University of Oklahoma. Oklahoma City—Maryjo Watson. Pawhuska—G. Daniel Boone,

E. Sean StandingBear, Osage Tribal Museum.
Texas: Canyon—Betty L. Bustos, Panhandle-Plains Historical Museum, Research Center. Lubbock—Mei Campbell, Henry Crawford, Museum of Texas Tech University. San Antonio—Martha Utterback, Daughters of the Republic of Texas, Texas History Research Library at the Alamo; Diane Bruce, The Institute of Texan Cultures.
Washington, D.C.: James Harwood, Vyrtis Thomas, National Anthropological Archives, Smithsonian Institution.

BIBLIOGRAPHY

BOOKS

Battey, Thomas C. *The Life and Adventures of a Quaker among the Indians.* Boston: Lee and Shepard, 1875.

Berlandier, Jean Louis. *The Indians of Texas in 1830.* Ed. by John C. Ewers. Washington, D.C.: Smithsonian Institution Press, 1969.

Bezy, John V., and Joseph P. Sanchez, eds. *Pecos, Gateway to Pueblos & Plains: The Anthology.* Tucson, Ariz.: Southwest Parks and Monuments Association, 1988.

Bolton, Herbert Eugene. *The Hasinais: Southern Caddoans as Seen by the Earliest Europeans.* Norman: University of Oklahoma Press, 1987.

Bolton, Herbert Eugene, ed. *Athanase de Mezieres and the Louisiana-Texas Frontier, 1768-1780.* 2 vols. Cleveland: Arthur H. Clark, 1914.

Boyd, Maurice. *Kiowa Voices: Myths, Legends and Folktales.* Vol. 2. Fort Worth: Texas Christian University Press, 1983.

Brant, Charles S., ed. *Jim Whitewolf: The Life of a Kiowa Apache Indian.* New York: Dover Publications, 1969.

The Buffalo Hunters, by the Editors of Time-Life Books (The American Indians series). Alexandria, Va.: Time-Life Books, 1993.

Capps, Benjamin, and the Editors of Time-Life Books. *The Great Chiefs* (The Old West series). Alexandria, Va.: Time-Life Books, 1975.

Catlin, George. *Letters and Notes on the Manners, Customs, and Conditions of the North American Indians.* Vol. 2. New York: Dover Publications, 1973.

Chalfant, William Y. *Dangerous Passage: The Santa Fe Trail and the Mexican War.* Norman: University of Oklahoma Press, 1994.

Chilton, Lance, et al. *New Mexico: A New Guide to the Colorful State.* Albuquerque: University of New Mexico Press, 1984.

Conn, Richard:
Circles of the World: Traditional Art of the Plains Indians. Denver: Denver Art Museum, 1982.
Native American Art in the Denver Art Museum. Denver: Denver Art Museum, 1979.

DeMallie, Raymond. "Touching the Pen." In *Ethnicity on the Great Plains.* Edited by Frederick C. Lubeke. Lincoln: University of Nebraska, 1980.

DeShields, James T. *Cynthia Ann Parker.* Dallas: Chalma Press, 1991.

Dobyns, Henry F. "Indians in the Colonial Spanish Borderlands." In *Indians in American History: An Introduction.* Arlington Heights, Ill.: Harlan Davidson, 1988.

Eastman, Edwin. *Seven and Nine Years among the Camanches and Apaches: An Autobiography.* Jersey City: Clark Johnson, 1873.

The European Challenge, by the Editors of Time-Life Books (The American Indians series). Alexandria, Va.: Time-Life Books, 1992.

Ewers, John Canfield:
Murals in the Round: Painted Tipis of the Kiowa and Kiowa-Apache Indians. Washington, D.C.: Smithsonian Institution Press, 1978.
Plains Indian Painting: A Description of an Aboriginal American Art. Stanford, Calif.: Stanford University Press, 1939.

Fehrenbach, T. R. *Comanches: The Destruction of a People.* New York: Alfred A. Knopf, 1974.

Foster, Morris W. *Being Comanche: A Social History of an American Indian Community.* Tucson: University of Arizona Press, 1991.

Garbarino, Merwyn S. *Native American Heritage.* Prospect Heights, Ill.: Waveland Press, 1985.

Gilles, Albert S. *Comanche Days.* Dallas: Southern Methodist University Press, 1974.

Hagan, William T.:
Quanah Parker, Comanche Chief. Norman: University of Oklahoma Press, 1993.
United States-Comanche Relations: The Reservation Years. New Haven, Conn.: Yale University Press, 1976.

Hagan, William T. "Squaw Men on the Kiowa, Comanche, and Apache Reservation: Advance Agents of Civilization or Disturbers of the Peace?" In *The Frontier Challenge.* Edited by John G. Clark. Lawrence: University of Kansas Press, 1971.

Haines, Francis:
Horses in America. New York: Thomas Y. Crowell, 1971.
The Plains Indians. New York: Thomas Y. Crowell, 1976.

Harris, Moira F. *Between Two Cultures: Kiowa Art from Fort Marion.* St. Paul: Pogo Press, 1989.

Hassrick, Royal B. *The George Catlin Book of American Indians.* New York: Promontory Press, 1988.

Holder, Preston. *The Hoe and the Horse on the Plains: A Study of Cultural Development among North American Indians.* Lincoln: University of Nebraska Press, 1970.

Hotz, Gottfried. *The Segesser Hide Paintings: Masterpieces Depicting Spanish Colonial New Mexico.* Trans. by Johannes Malthaner. Santa Fe: Museum of New Mexico Press, 1970.

Hoxie, Frederick E., ed. *Indians in American History: An Introduction.* Arlington Heights, Ill.: Harlan Davidson, 1988.

John, Elizabeth A. H. *Storms Brewed in Other Men's Worlds: The Confrontation of Indians, Spanish, and French in the Southwest, 1540-1795.* College Station: Texas A & M University Press, 1975.

Jones, David E. *Sanapia: Comanche Medicine Woman.* New York: Holt, Rinehart and Winston, 1972.

Jones, William K. *Notes on the History and Material Culture of the Tonkawa Indians.* Washington, D.C.: Smithsonian Press, 1969.

Kenner, Charles L. *A History of New Mexican-Plains Indian Relations.* Norman: University of Oklahoma Press, 1969.

Kessell, John L. *The Missions of New Mexico Since 1776.* Albuquerque: University of New Mexico Press, 1980.

Kestler, Frances Roe, comp. *The Indian Captivity Narrative: A Woman's View.* New York: Garland Publishing, 1990.

La Barre, Weston. *The Peyote Cult.* Hamden, Conn.: The Shoe String Press, 1964.

Leckie, William H. *The Military Conquest of the Southern Plains.* Norman: University of Oklahoma Press, 1963.

Lee, Nelson. *Three Years among the Comanches: The Narrative of Nelson Lee, the Texas Ranger.* Norman: University of Oklahoma Press, 1957.

Loomis, Noel M., and Abraham P. Nasatir. *Pedro Vial and the Roads to Santa Fe.* Norman: University of Oklahoma Press, 1967.

Lowie, Robert H.:
Indians of the Plains. New York: American Museum of Natural History, 1954.
"Societies of the Kiowa." In *Anthropological Papers of the American Museum of Natural History.* Vol. 11. New York: Published by Order of the Trustees, 1916.

Marriott, Alice:
Kiowa Years: A Study in Culture Impact. New York: Macmillan, 1968.
The Ten Grandmothers. Norman: University of Oklahoma Press, 1945.

Mathews, John Joseph. *The Osages: Children of the Middle Waters.* Norman: University of Oklahoma Press, 1961.

Mayhall, Mildred P. *The Kiowas.* Norman: University of Oklahoma Press, 1962.

McCoy, Ronald. *Kiowa Memories: Images from Indi-*

an Territory, 1880. Santa Fe, N. Mex.: Morning Star Gallery, 1987.

Methvin, J. J. *Andele or the Mexican-Kiowa Captive.* New York: Garland Publishing, 1976 (reprint of 1899 edition).

The Mighty Chieftains, by the Editors of Time-Life Books (The American Indians series). Alexandria, Va.: Time-Life Books, 1993.

Momaday, N. Scott. *The Way to Rainy Mountain.* Albuquerque: University of New Mexico Press, 1969.

Morse, Jedediah. *A Report to the Secretary of War of the United States on Indian Affairs.* New York: Augustus M. Kelley, 1970 (reprint of 1822 edition).

Nevin, David, and the Editors of Time-Life Books. *The Texans* (The Old West series). New York: Time-Life Books, 1975.

Newcomb, W. W., Jr. *The Indians of Texas: From Prehistoric to Modern Times.* Austin: University of Texas Press, 1961.

Newkumet, Vynola Beaver, and Howard L. Meredith. *Hasinai: A Traditional History of the Caddo Confederacy.* College Station: Texas A & M University Press, 1988.

Norall, Frank. *Bourgmont, Explorer of the Missouri, 1698-1725.* Lincoln: University of Nebraska Press, 1988.

Noyes, Stanley. *Los Comanches: The Horse People, 1751-1845.* Albuquerque: University of New Mexico Press, 1993.

Nuttall, Thomas. *A Journal of Travels into the Arkansa Territory.* Ann Arbor, Mich.: University Microfilms, 1966.

Nye, Wilbur Sturtevant. *Plains Indian Raiders.* Norman: University of Oklahoma Press, 1968.

O'Brien, Sharon. *American Indian Tribal Governments.* Norman: University of Oklahoma Press, 1989.

Petersen, Karen Daniels. *Plains Indian Art from Fort Marion.* Norman: University of Oklahoma Press, 1971.

Plummer, Rachel. *The Rachel Plummer Narrative.* Palestine, Tex.: n.p., 1926.

Plummer, Zula. *The Search for Rachel.* Private printing: Zula Plummer, 1976.

Richardson, Rupert Norval. *The Comanche Barrier to South Plains Settlement.* Glendale, Calif.: Arthur H. Clark, 1933.

Rollings, Willard H.:
 The Comanche. New York: Chelsea House Publishers, 1989.
 The Osage: An Ethnohistorical Study of Hegemony on the Prairie-Plains. Columbia: University of Missouri, 1992.

Schilz, Jodye Lynn Dickson, and Thomas F. Schilz. *Buffalo Hump and the Penateka Comanches* (Southwestern Studies series #88). El Paso: University of Texas, 1989.

Secoy, Frank. *Changing Military Patterns on the Great Plains.* Locust Valley, N.Y.: J. J. Augustin Publishers, 1953.

Simmons, Marc. *New Mexico: A Bicentennial History.* New York: W. W. Norton, 1977.

Simpson, Harold B. *Cry Comanche: The 2nd U.S. Cavalry in Texas, 1855-1861.* Hillsboro, Tex.: Hill Junior College Press, 1979.

Smith, Clinton L., and Jefferson D. Smith. *The Boy Captives: Life among the Indians.* Ed. by J. Marvin Hunter. New York: Garland Publishing, 1977 (reprint of 1927 edition).

Spencer, Robert F., and Jesse D. Jennings. *The Native Americans.* New York: Harper & Row, 1977.

Spielmann, Katherine A., ed. *Farmers, Hunters, and Colonists: Interaction between the Southwest and the Southern Plains.* Tucson: University of Arizona Press, 1991.

Stanley, F. *Satanta and the Kiowas.* Borger, Tex.: Jim Hess Printers, 1968.

Stewart, Omer C. *Peyote Religion: A History.* Norman: University of Oklahoma Press, 1987.

Terrell, John Upton. *The Plains Apache.* New York: Thomas Y. Crowell, 1975.

Thomas, Alfred Barnaby, ed. and trans. *After Coronado: Spanish Exploration Northeast of New Mexico, 1696-1727.* Norman: University of Oklahoma Press, 1935.

Tixier, Victor. *Tixier's Travels on the Osage Prairie.* Ed. by John Francis McDermott, translated by Albert J. Salvan. Norman: University of Oklahoma Press, 1940.

Utley, Robert M. *Frontier Regulars: The United States Army and the Indian, 1866-1891.* New York: Macmillan, 1973.

Waldman, Carl:
 Atlas of the North American Indian. New York: Facts On File, 1985.
 Encyclopedia of Native American Tribes. New York: Facts On File, 1988.

Wallace, Ernest, and E. Adamson Hoebel. *The Comanches: Lords of the South Plains.* Norman: University of Oklahoma Press, 1952.

War for the Plains, by the Editors of Time-Life Books (The American Indians series). Alexandria, Va.: Time-Life Books, 1993.

Webb, Walter Prescott:
 The Great Plains. Waltham, Mass.: Blaisdell, 1959.
 The Texas Rangers: A Century of Frontier Defense. Austin: University of Texas Press, 1965.

Weber, David J. *The Spanish Frontier in North America.* New Haven, Conn.: Yale University Press, 1992.

Weddle, Robert S. *The San Sabá Mission: Spanish Pivot in Texas.* Austin: University of Texas Press, 1964.

White, Richard. *The Roots of Dependency: Subsistence, Environment, and Social Change among the Choctaws, Pawnees, and Navajos.* Lincoln: University of Nebraska Press, 1983.

Wilbarger, J. W. *Indian Depredations in Texas.* Austin, Tex.: Steck, 1935 (reprint of 1889 edition).

Wunder, John R. *The Kiowa.* New York: Chelsea House Publishers, 1989.

PERIODICALS

Flores, Dan. "Bison Ecology and Bison Diplomacy: The Southern Plains from 1800 to 1850." *The Journal of American History,* September 1991.

Hodge, Frederick. "French Intrusion toward New Mexico in 1695." *New Mexican Historical Review,* 1929, vol. 4.

Opler, Marvin K. "The Origins of Comanche and Ute." *American Anthropologist,* 1943, vol. 45.

Rich, E. E. "Trade Habits and Economic Motivation among the Indians of North America." *Canadian Journal of Economics and Political Science,* February 1960.

Scott, Hugh Lenox. "Notes on the Kado, or Sun Dance of the Kiowa." *American Anthropologist,* July-September 1911.

Wedel, Mildred Mott:
 "Claude-Charles Dutisné: A Review of His 1719 Journeys." Part 1. *Great Plains Journal,* Fall 1972.
 "Claude-Charles Dutisné: A Review of His 1719 Journeys." Part 2. *Great Plains Journal,* Spring 1973.
 "J.-B. Bénard de la Harpe: Visitor to the Wichitas in 1719." *Great Plains Journal,* Spring 1971.

Wheelock, T. W. "Colonel Henry Dodge and His Regiment of Dragoons on the Plains in 1834." *Annals of Iowa,* January 1930.

Wiedman, Dennis. "Staff, Fan, Rattle and Drum: Spiritual and Artistic Expressions of Oklahoma Peyotists." *American Indian Art,* Summer 1985.

Wiedman, Dennis, and Candace Greene. "Early Kiowa Peyote Ritual and Symbolism: The 1891 Drawing Books of Silverhorn (Haungooah)." *American Indian Art,* Autumn 1988.

OTHER SOURCES

Maurer, Evan M. "Visions of the People: A Pictorial History of Plains Indian Life." Catalog. Minneapolis: Minneapolis Institute, 1992.

PICTURE CREDITS

The sources for the illustrations that appear in this book are listed below. Credits from left to right are separated by semicolons; from top to bottom they are separated by dashes.

Cover: National Anthropological Archives (NAA), Smithsonian Institution, no. 1426-B. **6, 7:** The Heard Museum; National Museum of American Art, Washington, D.C./Art Resource, N.Y. **8, 9:** National Museum of American Art, Washington, D.C./Art Resource, N.Y. (2); The National Museum of Denmark, Department of Ethnography, photography by Kit Weiss; courtesy National Museum of the American Indian, Smithsonian Institution, cat. no. 4/5266. **10, 11:** National Museum of American Art, Washington, D.C./Art Resource, N.Y.; Panhandle- Plains Historical Museum, Research Center, Canyon, Tex.—courtesy National Museum of the American Indian, Smithsonian Institution, cat. no. 20/3551. **12, 13:** Courtesy Museum of Texas Tech University, Lubbock, Tex., photography by Nicky Olson; National Museum of American Art, Washington, D.C./Art Resource, N.Y. **14, 15:** Panhandle-Plains Historical Museum, Research Center, Canyon, Tex.—National Museum of American Art,

Washington, D.C./Art Resource, N.Y. (2). **16:** NAA, Smithsonian Institution, no. 1782-K. **19:** Map by Maryland CartoGraphics, Inc. **22-26:** Jim Zintgraff, except pebble on p. 23, courtesy The Witte Museum, San Antonio. **28:** Courtesy National Museum of the American Indian, Smithsonian Institution, cat. no. 17/4177. **29:** National Gallery of Art, Washington, D.C., no. 1965.16.340. **30:** NAA, Smithsonian Institution, nos. 1352-A—34729-A. **32, 33:** NAA, Smithsonian Institution, nos. 1353-B—1353-C. **36, 37:** San Diego Museum of Man, photography by John Oldenkamp—Archives and Manuscripts Division of the Oklahoma Historical Society, no. 3523; courtesy Osage Tribal Museum, Pawhuska, Okla., photography by Don Wheeler (2). **38-39:** NAA, Smithsonian Institution, nos. 1729-A; 1369-A; 47999. **40:** Courtesy Osage Tribal Museum, Pawhuska, Okla., copied by Don Wheeler; NAA, Smithsonian Institution, no. 42931-B. **41:** Western History Collections, University of Oklahoma Library; NAA, Smithsonian Institution, no. 1782-C. **42:** Western History Collections, University of Oklahoma Library; Archives and Manuscripts Division of the Oklahoma Historical Society, no. 7482. **43:** NAA, Smithsonian Institution, no. 1767-A. **44:** Collection Musée de l'Homme, Cliché Paul Coze. **46:** David T. Vernon, Indian Arts Collection, Grand Teton National Park. **47:** Collection of the New-York Historical Society. **48, 49:** Institute of Texan Cultures, San Antonio; Larry Sherer, cat. no. 203781, Department of Anthropology, Smithsonian Institution. **50:** Map by Maryland CartoGraphics, Inc. **52-56:** Western History Collections, University of Oklahoma Library. **58:** Courtesy Morning Star Gallery, Santa Fe, N.Mex., photography by Addison Doty. **59:** Denver Art Museum, acc. no. 1937.41; Western History Collections, University of Oklahoma Library. **61:** NAA, Smithsonian Institution, no. 92-10307. **62:** Cat. no. 245023, Department of Anthropology, Smithsonian Institution. **63:** NAA, Smithsonian Institution, no. 55756; photography by Kirkpatrick Center Museum Complex, Oklahoma City, courtesy Department of Anthropology, Smithsonian Institution. **64, 65:** Cat. no. 245045, Department of Anthropology, Smithsonian Institution; NAA, Smithsonian Institution, no. P-55-B—cat. no. 245079, Department of Anthropology, Smithsonian Institution. **66, 67:** Courtesy Morning Star Gallery, Santa Fe, N.Mex.; cat. no. 245014, Department of Anthropology, Smithsonian Institution. **68, 69:** Cat. no. 245001, Department of Anthropology, Smithsonian Institution—Archives and Manuscripts Division of the Oklahoma Historical Society, neg. no. 2530; courtesy Morning Star Gallery, Santa Fe, N.Mex. **70, 71:** Cat. no. 245024, Department of

Anthropology, Smithsonian Institution; courtesy Morning Star Gallery, Santa Fe, N.Mex. **72:** National Museum of American Art, Washington, D.C./Art Resource, N.Y. **74:** Laurie Platt Winfrey, Inc., Archivo General de Indias, Seville. **76:** Courtesy John Carter Brown Library at Brown University. **77:** Daughters of the Republic of Texas, Texas History Research Library at the Alamo, San Antonio. **78, 79:** Yves Debraine, courtesy Museum of New Mexico. **80, 81:** Neg. no. 335481 (photo by Logan), courtesy Department of Library Services, American Museum of Natural History—neg. no. 324010, courtesy Department of Library Services, American Museum of Natural History. **82:** Photo courtesy The Edward E. Ayer Collection, Newberry Library. **84, 85:** © George H. H. Huey. **86, 87:** Dana B. Chase, courtesy Museum of New Mexico, no. 57017. **88, 89:** National Museum of American Art, Washington, D.C./Art Resource, N.Y.; Denver Art Museum, acc. no. 1956.10. **90:** Courtesy National Museum of the American Indian, Smithsonian Institution, neg. no. 36018. **92, 93:** Manuel Romero de Terreros/Unam. **94, 95:** NAA, Smithsonian Institution, nos. 1773-A; cat. no. 69-68, Department of Anthropology, Smithsonian Institution—© 1993 Walter Tutsi Wai BigBee. **96, 97:** Courtesy Museum of New Mexico, nos. 14297; 12378. **100, 101:** © Gilcrease Museum, Tulsa, Okla. **102:** National Museum of American Art, Washington, D.C./Art Resource, N.Y. **103:** Paulus Leeser, courtesy McElhaney Collection, U.S. Army Field Artillery and Fort Sill Museum. **104:** National Museum of American Art, Washington, D.C./Art Resource, N.Y. **106, 107:** NAA, Smithsonian Institution, no. 30750; Collection of Dwayne K. Davis, courtesy Pogo Press Inc. **108, 109:** Missouri Historical Society, acc. nos. 1882.18.5—1882.18.37; 1882.18.12. **110, 111:** Missouri Historical Society, acc. nos. 1882.18.3—1882.18.33; 1882.18.1. **112, 113:** Missouri Historical Society, acc. no. 1882.18.38. **114, 115:** Missouri Historical Society, acc. nos. 1882.18.8; 1882.18.39; 1882.18.30; 1882.18.44. **116, 117:** Missouri Historical Society, acc. nos. 1882.18.46; 1882.18.36. **118, 119:** Lloyd Rule, courtesy Denver Art Museum; NAA, Smithsonian Institution, no. 1459-B; © Dr. John D. Cunningham/Visual Unlimited. **120:** Panhandle-Plains Historical Museum, Research Center, Canyon, Tex. (2); Lloyd Rule, courtesy Denver Art Museum. **121:** Denver Art Museum, acc. no. 1950.104; Lloyd Rule, courtesy Denver Art Museum; Denver Art Museum, acc. no. 1953.366. **122:** NAA, Smithsonian Institution, no. 57058—Field Museum, Chicago, no. A110830.129c. **123:** Field

Museum, Chicago, no. A110830.114c—NAA, Smithsonian Institution, no. 94-12013. **124, 125:** Field Museum, Chicago, nos. A110830.122c—A110830.121c—A110830.120c; NAA, Smithsonian Institution, no. 1456-D; Field Museum, Chicago, no. A110830.123c. **126:** © 1993 Walter Tutsi Wai BigBee (2)—Oklahoma Museum of Natural History, University of Oklahoma, Norman. **127:** Courtesy Osage Tribal Museum, Pawhuska, Okla., photography by Don Wheeler—Jean-Loup Charmet, Paris. **128, 131:** NAA, Smithsonian Institution, nos. 1747-A-1; 1404-A. **132, 133:** National Museum of American Art, Washington, D.C./Art Resource, N.Y. **134, 135:** The Granger Collection, N.Y.; courtesy National Firearms Museum, photography by Steven H. Heyl. **138:** Photography by Roger Fry, courtesy The Witte Museum, San Antonio—The Institute of Texan Cultures, San Antonio, no. 68-71. **139:** NAA, Smithsonian Institution, no. 1735. **140:** Map by Maryland CartoGraphics, Inc. **143:** NAA, Smithsonian Institution, no. T-13409—courtesy Osage Tribal Museum, Pawhuska, Okla., photography by Don Wheeler (4). **144-145:** Courtesy Osage Tribal Museum, Pawhuska, Okla., photography by Don Wheeler (12). **146:** NAA, Smithsonian Institution, no. 4130-A—courtesy Osage Tribal Museum, Pawhuska, Okla., photography by Don Wheeler (2). **147:** Neg. no. 316873 (photo by Dixon), courtesy Department of Library Services, American Museum of Natural History—courtesy Osage Tribal Museum, Pawhuska, Okla., photography by Don Wheeler (2). **149:** Texas Memorial Museum, acc. no. 404-14. **150, 151:** Kansas State Historical Society, Topeka. **152:** Missouri Historical Society, acc. no. 1882.18.32. **154, 155:** The Granger Collection, N.Y.; NAA, Smithsonian Institution, nos. 1741-A; 1381-B; 1380-A; courtesy History Division, Seaver Center, Los Angeles County Museum of Natural History. **156, 157:** Panhandle-Plains Historical Museum, Research Center, Canyon, Tex.; © Walter Tutsi Wai BigBee. **158:** NAA, Smithsonian Institution, no. 1382-A-3. **160, 161:** Collection of H. Malcolm Grimmer, Santa Fe, N.Mex., photography by Addison Doty; NAA, Smithsonian Institution, no. 56376. **162:** Archives and Manuscripts Division of the Oklahoma Historical Society, no. 3773—NAA, Smithsonian Institution, no. 1754-A-2. **163:** NAA, Smithsonian Institution, no. 1748-B. **165:** Courtesy Texas State Archives. **166:** © 1993 Walter Tutsi Wai BigBee. **167:** © 1994 Walter Tutsi Wai BigBee. **168-173:** © 1993 Walter Tutsi Wai BigBee. **174:** © 1994 Walter Tutsi Wai BigBee. **175:** © 1993 Walter Tutsi Wai BigBee. **176, 177:** © 1992 Walter Tutsi Wai BigBee; © 1994 Walter Tutsi Wai BigBee.

INDEX

Numerals in italics indicate an illustration of the subject mentioned.